Dimensional Bead Embroidery

LARK JEWELRY
& BEADING

Dimensional Bead Embroidery

a reference guide to techniques

Jamie Cloud Eakin

LARK CRAFTS
Asheville

Editor
Nathalie Mornu

Development Editor
Ray Hemachandra

Copy Editor
Joe Rhatigan

Editorial Assistance
Abby Haffelt

Art Director
Kathleen Holmes

Art Production
Celia Naranjo

Junior Designer
Carol Barnao

Illustrator
Jamie Cloud Eakin

Photographer
Stewart O'Shields

Cover Designer
Celia Naranjo

Library of Congress Cataloging-in-Publication Data

Eakin, Jamie Cloud.
  Dimensional bead embroidery : a reference guide to techniques / Jamie Cloud Eakin.
      p. cm.
  Includes index.
  ISBN 978-1-60059-796-1 (hc-plc : alk. paper)
  1. Beadwork. 2. Bead embroidery. 3. Jewelry making. I. Title.
  TT860.E26 2011
  739.27--dc22

                          2011000674

10 9 8 7 6 5 4 3

Published by Lark Crafts
An Imprint of Sterling Publishing Co., Inc.
387 Park Avenue South, New York, NY 10016

Text © 2011, Jamie Cloud Eakin
Photography © 2011, Lark Crafts, an Imprint of Sterling Publishing Co., Inc.
Illustrations © 2011, Jamie Cloud Eakin

Distributed in Canada by Sterling Publishing,
c/o Canadian Manda Group, 165 Dufferin Street
Toronto, Ontario, Canada M6K 3H6

Distributed in the United Kingdom by GMC Distribution Services,
Castle Place, 166 High Street, Lewes, East Sussex, England BN7 1XU

Distributed in Australia by Capricorn Link (Australia) Pty Ltd.,
P.O. Box 704, Windsor, NSW 2756 Australia

If you have questions or comments about this book, please contact:
Lark Crafts
67 Broadway
Asheville, NC 28801
828-253-0467

Manufactured in China

For information about custom editions, special sales, premium, and corporate purchases, please contact the Sterling Special Sales Department at 800-805-5489 or specialsales@sterlingpub.com.

For information about desk and examination copies available to college and university professors, submit requests to academic@larkbooks.com. Our complete policy can be found at www.larkcrafts.com.

Contents

Introduction

THIS BOOK EXPLORES THE USE OF BEAD EMBROIDERY STITCHES to create fabulous beadwork. I'll show you how to use old stitches in new ways and add some new techniques to push the boundaries and create a new dimension in bead embroidery.

We'll explore common bead embroidery stitches and add some new ones. Surface stitches are the mainstay of bead embroidery, but as they say, it's not over 'til it's over. So I'll introduce methods for embellishing the edges of a bead-embroidered piece. We'll also explore combination techniques that can take bead embroidery from a surface design to a piece of jewelry, a wall hanging, a purse, and beyond.

At the back of the book, I give you nine projects with step-by-step instructions. These allow you to put the techniques from the previous sections into practice with some guidance. There are also numerous photos of other designs throughout the book. Photo descriptions (page 154) for these list the techniques and stitches used for each piece. You can use them as inspiration for creating an infinite number of your own unique and fabulous designs.

I think my favorite thing about bead embroidery is not only the capacity for variety but also the simplicity. Even if you can barely sew on a button, you can do this.

So get ready, get set, and go forth and create.

Jamie

CHAPTER 1

Materials and Tools

In this chapter, you'll find all the information you need about beads and components for your designs and the tools you ought to have on hand.

tip Purchase the same color of bead in sizes 15°, 11°, 8°, and 6°. It's often useful to have a selection of bead sizes of the same color to fit into a space as you're covering a surface.

Seed Beads

Seed beads, small glass beads named for the seeds they resemble, are used throughout the projects. They're round in appearance and are also referred to as *rocailles*. There are also seed beads, such as Delicas and Tohos, that were created especially for loom and other weaving stitches. These beads are more cylindrical in shape and therefore not as versatile for bead embroidery.

Seed beads are sized according to number; the higher the number, the smaller the bead. The most common size seed bead is size 11°. (Seed bead size is indicated by a number followed by the degree symbol, which is pronounced "ott," or by a slash and a zero: 11/0.)

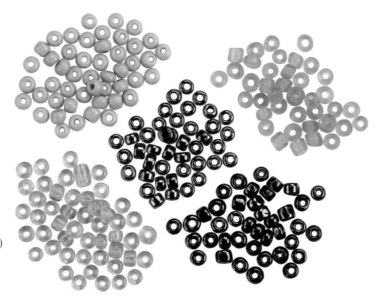

Other Beads and Components

A bead is anything that has a hole through it so it can be sewn on, strung, or woven.

Meanwhile, a component is anything else that you wish to incorporate into your designs but that doesn't have holes. This includes cabochons (which are stones, gems, or other objects that have a flat back and a smooth, domed surface), rivolis, buttons, donuts, etc. Beads and components may be created from man-made materials, such as glass and acrylics, or from natural materials, such as genuine stones, shells, and more.

When selecting your beads and components, you need to consider the function of the end piece. It's generally easier to choose beads and components for jewelry than it is for garments and home interior items because many beads are sensitive to excessive sun exposure or cleaning agents. It can be difficult to determine these sensitivities because dyes and coated finishes on beads are so pervasive and done so well that you can't tell by simply looking at them. Accordingly, the best method is to test a sampling of the beads and components by using typical cleaners on them and exposing them to sunlight.

I also encourage you to create your beadwork independent of the item you're working on so that the beadwork can be removed when, say, a garment needs to be washed. Apply an attachment method that suits the item, such as sew-on snaps, hooks, or Velcro. This is also helpful because your beadwork will probably last longer than any garment, anyway!

Needles

Beading needles are different from regular sewing needles: they're much thinner and the eye is smaller. They're made specifically for beading and are labeled "beading needles." I prefer English-made needles because they tend to have a larger thread hole in relation to the needle size. Beading needles come in sizes 10, 12, 13, and up—the higher the number, the smaller the needle. For most of the embroidery in this book, I suggest you use a size 12 beading needle.

Beading needles also come in different lengths. The standard is a 2-inch (5 cm) needle; however, shorter needles—usually 1 inch (2.5 cm) long and referred to as *sharps*—are useful for difficult backings, such as stiff leathers. Long needles, up to 4 inches (10.2 cm), are also available and are useful when working with long beads.

Thread

Use beading thread in your bead embroidery projects; *don't* use embroidery and sewing threads, which are too weak to support beadwork. Beading thread comes in various colors and is generally made from nylon (such as Nymo) or a rice filament (such as Silamide), and may be prewaxed. Threads are sized with an alphabetic designation, such as A, B, C, O, etc. Use size A or B for the projects in this book. The choice of beading thread, whether Nymo, Silamide, or a similar thread product, is a personal preference and any will be satisfactory.

Backing Materials

There are two categories of backings used in bead embroidery. One is the under-backing (frequently just referred to as "the backing"), the surface onto which the beads are sewn. The other is the outer-backing, which is used in the final stages to cover the back of the bead-embroidered piece and protect the stitches. Basically, anything you can sew through is a potential backing, although fabrics and leathers are the most popular choices. Your choice of fabrics includes fused, woven, and leather; a full discussion of these can be found on page 17.

Stabilizers

There are times when a project requires more stiffness, strength, or stability than is provided by the backings and beads. You can add this by inserting a stabilizer between the under-backing and the outer-backing. Flashing is a thin metal used in home roof construction, available at hardware stores. It's very thin but stiff, and can easily be cut with tin snips or a pair of heavy, strong scissors. It's a great stabilizer, especially for post-style earrings or pins. Flat plastic sheets cut from an empty milk or juice carton are also useful.

Creating a Stabilizer

To create a stabilizer, first make a paper pattern. Trace the embroidered piece and cut the paper approximately ³/₁₆ inch (5 mm) in from the traced edge. Lay the pattern on the flashing or plastic, trace, and cut out. Measure the stabilizer against the actual beaded piece and trim if needed. Be sure to leave space around the edge so that any edge stitching later applied is not affected. Also leave blank any other area that will have more stitches applied. Then glue the flashing to the under-backing. When the glue is dry, apply the outer-backing.

Findings

The clasps, jump rings, head pins, and other hardware used in jewelry creations are called *findings*. Most bead stores carry a vast variety of such hardware in metals ranging from inexpensive plated brass to more costly sterling silver, gold-filled, and gold.

CLASPS

Clasps provide a mechanism to open and close necklaces and bracelets. There are dozens of styles and types, such as hook and eye, hook and chain, toggle, spring ring, magnetic, and more. Most types are suitable for all uses; however, hook-and-eye clasps shouldn't be used for bracelets because the clasp can open easily, allowing the bracelet to fall off.

JUMP RINGS

Jump rings are small wire circles that join beadwork to some other kind of finding, such as a clasp. The ring has a slit in it that can be opened. You open the ring, insert it through the loop on the clasp and the loop on the beadwork, and then close the ring. Be careful not to open the jump ring by spreading the ends outward

and enlarging the circle. This will weaken the ring and destroy the roundness. Instead, with a pair of pliers in each hand, twist the ring open by pushing one end forward and the other end backward. Close in the same manner, reversing the direction.

PIN BACKS

Most pin findings have a thin strip of metal used to glue the finding onto a jewelry project. Because the pin finding (or *pin back*) will be glued to fabric or leather in the projects in this book, there are significant issues in terms of strength. To compensate for this, the best method is to "enlarge" the surface area that will be glued to the bead embroidery backing.

1 Draw an outline of the project on a piece of paper.

2 Create a pattern from the outline, cutting approximately ³⁄₁₆ inch (5 mm) from the outer edge.

3 Place the pattern on a piece of flashing (photo below) or other metal, trace, and cut the form from the metal.

4 Glue the pin back onto the flashing using a good metal-to-metal glue (usually an epoxy works best).

5 When dry, attach the flashing to the under-backing of the bead embroidery piece using an all-purpose, flexible glue (see Glue on page 13).

6 Apply the outer-backing, cutting holes in it to accommodate the pin.

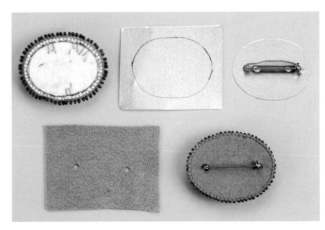

EAR WIRES AND POSTS

Posts, wires, clip-on findings—most of the types seen on commercial earrings are available to beaders, too. With *drop-type* earring findings, the mechanism has a loop used to attach to the beadwork. As with jump rings, *don't* open it by spreading out the ends of the loop; instead, use a pair of pliers in each hand and twist open the loop, insert the beadwork, and twist to close. With *post-type* findings, there's a post "pad" that's glued to the beadwork. This can present strength problems similar to when adding a pin back (page 11). The solution used for pins works great for post earrings, too.

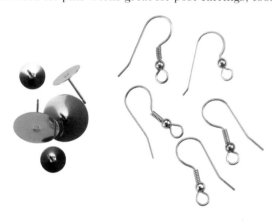

The Toolbox

All of these tools are used in creating beadwork and are available in most bead and/or crafts stores and on the Internet.

SCISSORS

Look for a small pair of scissors with sharp blades—you want a pair that's easy to handle. Additionally, a pair of curved manicure scissors is very useful for trimming.

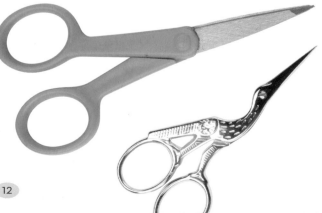

EMBROIDERY HOOPS

Embroidery hoops are available in many sizes. Use them to hold the fabric or backing taut while sewing. The issue with using hoops when embroidering with beads is that the hoop can't fit over a fabric area that has a bead sewn on it. However, these can be useful when using a flexible backing such as a loose fabric and when the design can fit inside the hoop.

MARKERS

Use markers to color the backing material, draw your design, or mark key spots on your backing. I recommend colorfast, permanent markers in both a fine tip (for drawing lines) and a wide tip (for coloring in areas).

PLIERS

You need two sets of pliers in your beading tool kit: needle nose and round nose. Pliers are used to attach ear wires and other findings to beadwork. Use one in each hand to open and close a jump ring. Use the round-nose pliers to shape findings into a circle or loop. If you purchase these from a hardware store, be sure to get small sizes that are easy to handle.

Needle-nose pliers

Round-nose pliers

WIRE CUTTERS

It's often necessary to trim the length of a head pin or other wire. Wire cutters known as side cutters are perfect for these purposes.

BEADING PAD

Made specifically for beading, these pads resemble a small fleece blanket with a nap like that of velvet. The pad provides a cushion that allows you to pour out small piles of beads that stay in place without rolling around. The beads sit on top of the fibers, making it much easier to pick them up with a needle.

Side cutter

WAX AND THREAD CONDITIONERS

Use beeswax and other thread conditioners to make bead thread more manageable. Some threads are pre-waxed and don't need any additional products. Base the use of these on individual preference.

LAMP

Good lighting is important for your comfort while beading. I recommend a small lamp that allows you to direct light at your work area. Several lamps are designed especially for beaders, with "true color" lightbulbs that help you select the right color beads.

Glue

The glue you use will depend on what you're gluing.

- Fabric to fabric: Fabric glues are available as washable and not washable. Read the labels, and select the glue suitable for your project.

- Metal to metal: If you're gluing a pin finding to metal flashing, use an epoxy (you mix the two parts together) that's specified for use with metal.

- One type of material to another (fabric to glass, fabric to metal, etc.): Use an all-purpose glue to apply glass, stone, wood, metal, etc. to the backing. Read the description on the label of the glue to determine what the glue is designed for. Make sure it includes both types of materials that you're gluing together. Also make sure the glue dries clear and is flexible.

tip

You can test an all-purpose glue by placing a small amount on a smooth, plastic surface such as the plastic from a milk container. After the glue dries overnight, try to pull it off. If the glue pops off quickly in one stroke, it's not very strong. If it requires a good tug and you need to keep pulling to remove every bit, then it's strong. Once the glue is removed, it should be bendable. If it breaks like a piece of glass, it isn't flexible and I don't recommend using it.

Materials for the Projects

Each of the projects lists the beads, components, tools, and other things needed to complete the project.

All of the projects call for seed beads. If a project calls for a size 11° seed bead, substituting another size bead is not recommended; however, you can use the following sizes interchangeably with the projects in this book: 14° and 15°; 8° and 9°; and 5° and 6°.

Note that for beading thread, I prefer Silamide or Nymo.

The projects also call for under-backing. (See page 10 for a full discussion of backings.) As a general rule, I prefer to use Lacy's Stiff Stuff for the under-backing. In all the projects, the beadwork covers the entire surface of the under-backing, so its color isn't critical. Lacy's Stiff Stuff is generally available only in white. When the beadwork is dark, I either dye the under-backing or use a permanent marker to color it so the bright white doesn't show through in between the beads. You can use any color as desired.

Outer-backing is incorporated in all of the projects. I generally use Ultrasuede. Because the outer-backing is completely hidden on the back side, its color isn't critical. As a general rule, I use a color that matches the Sunshine Edge beads. However, any color will work.

CHAPTER 2

Basic Techniques

Learn the techniques used in many beading projects,
including bead embroidery projects.

Adding Stop Beads

Starting a beadwork project often involves leaving the tail thread for use later in completing the beadwork. Therefore, there are no beginning knots to hold the tension. The use of a stop bead compensates for this and helps hold the tension in the thread. You use the stop bead temporarily and later remove it. The best stop bead is a size 8° or 9° bead in a matte finish. The roughness of the matte finish helps hold the thread better, and the larger size makes the bead easier to remove later. However, any bead can be used as a stop bead.

1 Pick up the bead and move it to the desired location.

2 Stitch through it so the thread is looped around the bead (figure 1). Be careful not to stitch through the thread already there (referred to as "piercing the thread"); otherwise, it will cause problems later.

3 Pull the thread so the loop wraps tightly around the bead.

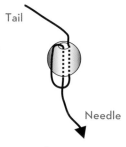

Tail

Needle

figure 1

Tying Knots

Knots are used at the end of stitching to secure threads before they're cut. There are two circumstances for knots. One is when two thread ends are available to tie a knot and the other is when only one thread is available.

TWO-THREAD KNOT (SQUARE KNOT)

This is the preferred situation because this knot is the most secure. When a square knot is tied correctly, any stress on the knot actually makes it tighter.

1 Position the thread ends so that they exit two different areas or beads—one thread on the right and the other on the left (figure 2a).

2 Loop the right over and around the left (figure 2b).

3 Then take the thread that's now on the left and loop it over and around the right (figure 2c).

4 Pull the ends to secure the knot (figure 2d).

5 If you want the knot even more secure, after step 4, repeat step 2 and pull tightly before weaving in the ends (figure 2e).

6 Weave one end into the beadwork (see below) in one direction. Weave the other end into the beadwork in the opposite direction, and then cut.

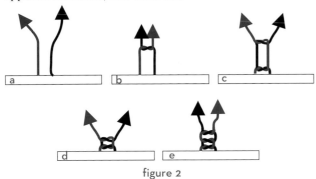

figure 2

ONE-THREAD KNOT

1 Stitch to an area in the beadwork where there are two threads coming out of a bead in two different directions. Stitch under the two threads and pull gently to create a loop (figure 3a). Or, if on a backing, stitch through the fabric to create a loop.

2 Stitch through the loop and then through the loop again (figures 3b and c).

3 Pull slowly to close the loops. Pull tight.

4 Weave in (see below), and then cut.

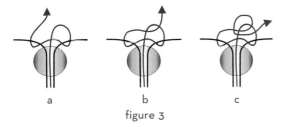

figure 3

HALF-HITCH KNOT

Perform this just like the one-thread knot, except on step 2, stitch through the loop only once. This knot isn't as bulky as the one-thread knot, and it's a good knot to use for securing thread tension while beading.

Weaving into Beadwork

Weave into the beadwork or backings before cutting the thread. Always cut thread away from the knot, not next to it. Fabric weavers have discovered that weaving threads back in actually eliminates the need for knots if the weaving is done up, then down, then up, then down. So knot and weave to produce a really secure thread end.

Finding and Marking Centers

Once you've completed a piece of bead embroidery, it's often necessary to perform other beading, such as adding a bail to attach to a necklace. If you want the bail to be centered, you need to find the center position on the edge row. Even if the piece is asymmetrical, the following method can be used to identify the spot where the area of one side is roughly equal to the area of the other side.

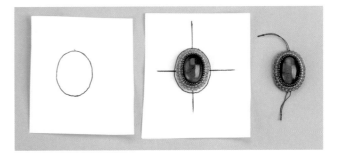

1 Put the work on a blank piece of paper. Use a dark pen to trace an outline (photo above, left).

2 Now hold the paper up to the light and fold it in half, matching up the outlines of each half. If asymmetrical, fold where the area of one side appears to be equal to the total area of the other side.

3 If desired, fold again (in fourths). Unfold the paper and mark the fold lines with the pen.

4 Place the work back on the paper (photo above, center). Use the folds to estimate the center top and center bottom. Mark by putting a spare needle at each of the center spots. Count the beads between the centers to verify (the bead counts on each side should be equal). Adjust as needed.

5 The center will either be a specific bead or between two beads. Tie a thread there to mark it (photo above, right). You'll remove this thread later; use it to temporarily keep track of the center spot(s).

CHAPTER 3

Getting Started and Designing

This chapter will take you through the steps needed for bead embroidery,

with chapters 5 through 8 focusing on the specific stitches and techniques

you use in steps 3, 7, and 8 described directly below.

The steps used for bead embroidery are generally the same for any project and include:

1 Plan your design.

2 Select and prepare your backing.

3 Sew the beads on according to your design.

4 Review the beaded piece.

5 Trim the under-backing.

6 Select and trim the outer-backing (and stabilizer, if needed) and attach it to the under-backing.

7 Bead the edges.

8 Do a final finishing, including combining, edge embellishments, and attaching.

Plan Your Design

There are many ways for the creative process to happen. The technique described here is easy to do, and you can adapt it to your individual style of creating. Generally, you'll have an idea of the type of project you want to do, whether a necklace, purse, earrings, pillow cover, and so on.

1 Start by gathering all of the beads and components that you may possibly include in your piece. Include all of the possibilities from small seed beads to large components.

2 Use a blank piece of paper to plan your design. Measure and create a pattern form. For instance, if the project is a pillow cover, measure and cut the paper for the pillow and test the size over the pillow form. Or, if

the project is a cuff bracelet, measure and cut the paper and test around the cuff to make sure the fit is correct.

3 If the piece is symmetrical, fold the pattern in half and cut so that each half is identical. Mark the center fold line. Measure again as described in step 2.

4 Now create a second pattern and set it aside.

5 Place the beads and components on your first pattern form to create your plan, moving and adjusting them until you have the design you like. Start with the largest beads and components or the most strategically important ones. Continue to place and move them around until only the seed beads remain to be added.

6 Move the beads and components one by one from the first to the second pattern and trace around the beads and components onto the second pattern as you go. Start with the largest or most strategically important ones first and continue until all parts of the design are transferred and traced (photo below). Your first pattern is now blank and available for use later if needed.

7 In the blank areas where seed beads will be stitched, make notes of the stitch type and color. You now have your pattern!

tip Take a digital photo of your layout and print out the picture for reference. This is also helpful as you develop your plan: take a picture, then move the beads into another design, take a new picture, and repeat. Later, select the picture you like best.

Select and Prepare Your Backing

The next step in bead embroidery is to select and prepare your under-backing, onto which you'll sew your beads.

BACKING MATERIALS

What you choose for your backing is a function of the design and, ultimately, up to you. Obviously, if you plan to cover the entire surface with beads, the selection process will be different than if you'll apply beads only to certain areas.

With bead embroidery stitches, the surface of the backing can be completely covered or not.

Fused Fabrics

The most popular fabric choices include those with a fused construction, such as Ultrasuede, felt, fused interfacing, and Lacy's Stiff Stuff, which is a fused fabric created specifically for bead embroidery. All of these have the advantage of having an edge that won't unravel the way woven fabrics tend to do. However, because stiffer backings hold heavy beads and components better, I recommend Lacy's Stiff Stuff for jewelry projects. (It also has the advantage of being very easy to stitch through.)

Woven Fabrics

Don't disregard woven fabrics simply because they can fray at the edges—they're an interesting choice for many bead embroidery projects such as purses, pillows, and wall hangings. You can treat the edges by sewing a hem during the final construction phase, applying fabric glue, or using one of the fabric treatments designed to stop edges from fraying. If your design calls for a woven fabric backing that's not completely covered with beads, consider using a fabric protector such as Scotchgard for easier cleaning. Apply this treatment before any beads are sewn on.

Leather

Leather is also popular and will not unravel. It can be difficult to stitch through depending on its weight, and care should also be taken with certain designs. Repeated, close stitches can create a perforated line in the leather, causing it to tear like perforated paper if stressed. For both these reasons, I don't recommend leather as a backing.

> **tip**
> If your chosen backing is too lightweight for the beads or design, consider doubling it. You can use spots of fabric glue to adhere two pieces together. Or, use one of the many iron-on fused interfacing products. Simply apply heat with an iron to melt the plastic/wax substance on the interfacing to fuse it to the backing. This will add to its stability and help stop any edges from fraying. Select the interfacing (available from lightweight to heavyweight) based on the desired stability. Test a small sample to make sure the backing and interfacing are compatible and that you can still easily get a needle through it. Let it cool completely before stitching to avoid gumming up your needle.

PREPARE THE BACKING

Make sure the backing is sufficient to hold the weight of the beads and components you've selected.

1 Trace the outline of your pattern onto the backing. If you're using a stiff, non-fray backing, you can cut along the outline now or after all sewing is done. If you're using a backing that frays and you want to cut out the pattern now, consider using a no-fray glue or treatment to the edges of the backing first.

> **tip**
> If your design has a specific shape, I recommend cutting it out at the beginning. It's usually easier to sew the beads near the edge than risk cutting threads when the shape is cut after beading.

2 Now carefully mark the first critical bead/component placements. One constant with designing bead embroidery is that plans often change as beads are applied. You have your original pattern or picture to refer to as you bead and you can mark additional placements as needed. Waiting to mark provides you with the ability to

> **tip**
> One solution is to mark the back side of the backing. Stitch on the marking lines with thread that matches the backing color, using a long Running Stitch (page 47). The thread line will be visible to you as you stitch on the beads but will not otherwise show.

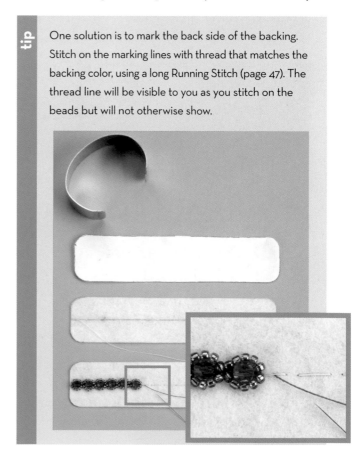

evolve the design as you see it taking shape. If desired, color in areas on the backing using permanent or color-fast markers, but only as needed.

Be careful marking the backing. For example, don't use a black pen on a white backing with light-colored, transparent beads. Even when completely covered with beads, the backing may show through in areas and it will impact the colors of the beads. The pen markings will show through the beads and spoil the finished piece.

3 Start sewing on the beads and components using the techniques in this chapter and in chapters 4 through 8. Select the largest and/or most strategically important ones first, and glue on and sew. Continue adding from large to small and create your design. Bead embroidery is like a building process. Continue to mark and color your under-backing as you bead, adjusting the spacing and design as needed.

tip If your plan includes a row (or rows) of beads between two components, sew on the row (or the key part of the row) before gluing the second component to get the placement just right (photo above).

Sew the Beads on According to Your Design

With the backing prepared, it's time to execute your design. Chapters 4 through 8 provide you with the necessary techniques. It's also helpful to review the projects on pages 89 to 141. Even if you don't plan on making the project itself, you'll gain valuable tips and knowledge on how to create a bead-embroidered piece.

Review the Beaded Piece

It's time to look over your beaded piece with a critical eye. Usually there's a spot or two (or even many more!) that needs one or more beads sewn in. Your design idea is now a beaded reality that you can love and move on—or you can modify it, add layers, or make any other changes you want. This is the time to make any adjustments, before the outer-backing is applied and adjustments are more difficult.

Trim the Under-Backing

In some cases, the under-backing is already trimmed, because you performed the beading on backing cut to the desired shape. If that's not the case, then you need to trim the backing. First, cut the backing, leaving a ⅛-inch-wide (3 mm) area around the beadwork. Then, look at the back side, which shows the stitching, and determine how close you can trim without cutting any threads. Continue to trim off the outside edges of the backing, without clipping any threads. Don't trim too close; as you look at the beadwork, you should see a sliver of under-backing around the edge.

Select and Trim the Outer-Backing and Attach It to the Under-Backing

In many instances (jewelry items are the most obvious example), a second backing (the outer-backing) is also required. Outer-backings are applied and sewn onto the back of a bead-embroidered piece after all the surface beads are applied to protect the underside of the stitches and provide a neat, clean appearance for the back of the piece. It's typical to include one when the piece is transformed into jewelry or if the back is exposed. Even if the piece will be mounted, you may want to add an outer-backing for the protection of stitches or for reinforcement and strength. The best outer-backings are fused fabrics, particularly Ultrasuede or a fused interfacing. The key is that the edges don't unravel like a woven fabric.

What You Do

1 Apply glue to the back side of the beaded under-backing. Start in the center and work out toward the edges, leaving an area ³⁄₁₆ inch (5 mm) wide glue-free around the entire edge. This area will be stitched later, and glue interferes with that process.

2 Press the outer-backing to the under-backing and let dry.

3 Trim the outer-backing to match the edge of the under-backing.

Bead the Edges

Once the outer-backing is glued and trimmed, it's time to permanently attach the outer-backing to the beaded under-backing. This is accomplished by beading around the edge, which will also stitch the two backings together. The primary methods for doing this are the Clean Edge on page 63 and the Sunshine Edge on page 64. While it's possible to stitch the backings together with a Whipstitch (page 47), I don't recommend this because it leaves the edges of the backings visible when viewing the piece from the side.

Do a Final Finishing

The steps you use for final finishing will depend on your design. These steps include adding edge embellishments, attaching bead strands and findings, and combining with other beaded pieces. Chapter 7 includes techniques for finishing edges that take your design to the next level of fabulous. Chapter 8 addresses attaching bead strands to complete a necklace, bracelet, etc. Combining beaded pieces is discussed below.

COMBINING BEADED PIECES

Beads, components, and various stitches are used in bead embroidery to add dimension to the beadwork. Dimension can also be added using combination techniques. In the pieces below, the first and third are examples of necklace pendants that use a consolidated backing. The second and fourth necklaces below are examples of pendants created as separate pieces and then stitched together (combined). The size and number of focal beads used are roughly the same in each, but the final results look very different.

Each method has advantages. Creating separate pieces makes it easier to add dimension using curves and deep indentations on the outline, as seen in the second and fourth examples in the photos below. However, the advantage of having the increased surface area of a single backing is that it's easier to add dimension with your bead and stitch selection.

Using separate pieces is the easiest way to add "cutout" areas in the beadwork, as in the three examples at the bottom of page 21. These cutout areas add another

dimension to the beadwork, and because they're more flexible, they're more comfortable to wear. Plus, the holes act as ventilation, so they're also cooler.

You can also use both methods (one-piece construction and separate pieces) as seen in the photos above.

COMBINING BEAD-EMBROIDERED PIECES

You can stitch the edge of one piece directly to the edge of another piece or you can add beads in between. The illustrations on the next two pages demonstrate a direct attachment. However, you can add a bead or beads in between the edge stitches, and the thread path is the same.

What You Do

1 Prepare the edge of each piece that's to be combined using the Sunshine Edge (page 64).

2 Using single thread, stitch up from the back side to the top side. Position the needle below one of the Sunshine Edge beads to be used and stitch at least ⅛ inch (3 mm) from the edge of the backings (figure 1). (All stitches that follow should be at least ⅛ inch [3 mm] from the edge of the backings, and more than that is actually better.) Look at the top side to see where the needle is positioned so you don't interfere with any beads there. Sew underneath those beads if needed to get to the Sunshine Edge bead.

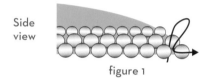

figure 1

3 Stitch out through the Sunshine Edge bead. Flip the two pieces so both face down. Pick up one bead (or none, or more, as desired). Stitch through the edge bead on the other piece, staying on the back side. Then stitch through the backing to the top side position, with the needle directly under the Sunshine Edge bead (figure 2).

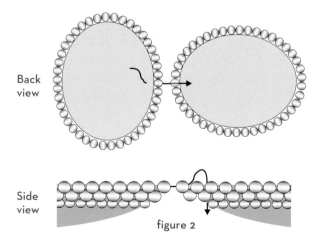

figure 2

4 Flip the pieces over so they face up. Stitch over to the next bead to be attached. Position the needle below the next Sunshine Edge bead and stitch through the backings to the back side (figure 3). This small stitch will be on the top side, hidden between the beads.

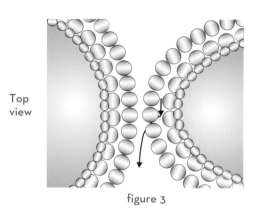

figure 3

5 Flip to the back side again. Stitch out through the Sunshine Edge bead. Pick up one bead (or none, or more, as desired). Stitch through the Sunshine Edge bead on the other piece, staying to the back side. Stitch through the backings to the top side (figure 4).

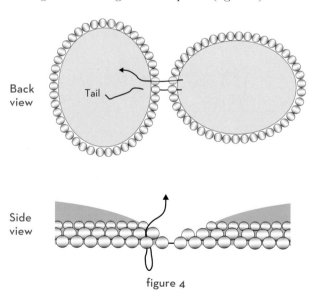

figure 4

6 Repeat steps 4 and 5 until you have the desired number of Sunshine Edge beads attached (figure 5).

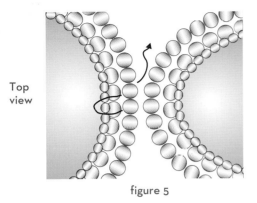

Top view

figure 5

7 To strengthen, repeat the stitch path, traveling back to the starting point. If there will be lots of pull or stress on the joined area, repeat the thread path a third time.

8 If needed, stitch over to the tail thread. Use the tail thread and needle thread to tie a square knot (page 14). Finally, weave in and cut.

Below are examples of different alignments from one Sunshine Edge to another and thread paths for each.

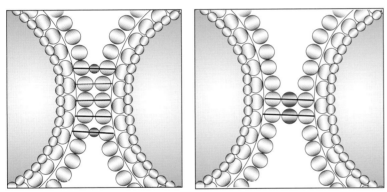

In the above examples, the beads on one piece directly line up with the other piece.

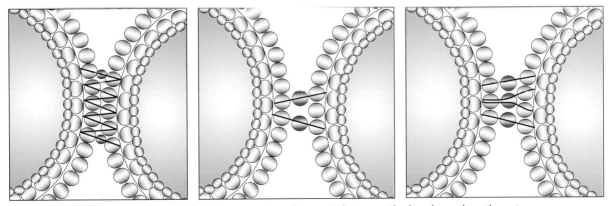

The examples above show how the beads on one piece line up in between the beads on the other piece.

CHAPTER 4

Using Components

One of the most important ways to add dimension to bead embroidery is incorporating non-bead items. With beads, attachment to the backing is obvious—the sewn thread holds the beads on. With other items (referred to as components), it's not always obvious. But, where there's a will, there's a way! This chapter features techniques to use on components and how to incorporate various components into bead embroidery.

To Glue or Not to Glue

If a component has a flat back, it can be glued onto the backing; however using *only* glue can be problematic in many circumstances. For instance, components glued to flexible backings, such as a cabochon on a fabric or leather purse, can pop off if pressure from the purse's contents bows the backing. A glue with insufficient holding strength will also create problems for a bracelet that receives normal bangs and knocks. Observe caution when using glue as the only solution for holding a component in place. Also, always test the glue before applying it, to make sure it doesn't react adversely to your component, especially if the component has a foil backing.

The techniques in this chapter don't rely solely on glue to hold the components on, and they're all bead embroidery stitch techniques rather than peyote, brick, or netting stitches. While those types of beadwork stitches can encase a component, they often cover more of the surface than bead embroidery techniques do. The component is often the star of the show, so it's desirable to use a stitch that holds it in place, yet covers less of its surface. Furthermore, with bead embroidery stitches, it's easier to introduce a design element into the stitch, so the practical aspect of encasing the component can be achieved while also adding a design touch.

Even though glue isn't the primary technique holding the component to the backing, it's usually used to hold the component in place while you apply the surrounding beadwork.

Uneven Components

Many components, such as cabochons and pendants, have flat bases, yet others don't have a sufficiently flat shape to enable you to glue the component down to hold it while you bead around it. These uneven surfaces can also be problematic if they move and wobble around. The solution is to create a flat base for the item, and the techniques below let you incorporate nearly anything you find into your design.

CREATE A FLAT BASE

To create a base, use clay. Clay is available in most craft stores in various colors and types. Look for a clay that will air-dry and is permanent when dry. The color isn't important—you can paint or dye it to achieve another color if you wish.

tip Components are not the only things to use here. Big rounded beads can benefit from this, creating a stable "cradle."

What You Do

1 Shape a small amount of clay. For buttons, roll and form a donut; for other components, shape a mound.

2 Place the clay on waxed paper or aluminum foil. Press the component down into the center of the clay, keeping it level.

3 With a razor or knife, trim or remove any excess along the edges. Let the clay dry overnight.

4 Lift the component off the clay mold. Trim any excess clay with sandpaper or carve with the razor or knife.

5 Seal the clay with clear nail polish, if desired. If the component is transparent, you can also paint the clay base to match your backing, using acrylic paint.

6 Put glue in the mold and replace the component. Let the glue dry.

Cabochons

A cabochon has a flat back and a domed top. Cabochons are available in natural materials, such as gemstones, and man-made materials, such as glass. Using cabochons is very popular in bead embroidery, and they're available in a variety of shapes, including round, oval, square, triangle, and irregular (a.k.a. designer shapes), and they come in many sizes, from very small (6 mm) to quite large (more than 80 mm). The main issue to resolve with cabochons is how to securely attach them to the beadwork. This is solved by creating a beaded bezel. Chapter 6 discusses how to accomplish the task.

> **tip** Flat top-drilled beads are like a combination of a bead (the top) and a cabochon (the bottom). Simply sewing the bead on will only secure the top of the bead. Treat the bottom part like a cabochon and use bezel stitches to securely attach it to the backing.

Pendants

Pendants come in many shapes and materials. If the back surface isn't flat, follow the Create a Flat Base instructions on page 25. Use a pin or toothpick to open up the pendant hole through the clay base. A pendant's hole is drilled from top to bottom versus side-drilled like a bead. In most cases, a visible hole could be considered a defect in your design. Below are some solutions.

COVER WITH A BEZEL

In chapter 6, I illustrate techniques that involve placing beads on top of the component. So, for example, the Bugle Row Bezel (page 56) can be placed so that it covers the hole. In the Abalone Necklace (below, right), there's a large hole beneath those bugle beads. The Flower Bezel (page 60) can be used in a similar manner, and if the hole is small enough, you may be able to use the Twisted Bezel (page 52 and photo below, left).

COVER WITH A BEAD

This is an easy solution for a small hole (photos above). The critical aspect is to sew the bead(s) on securely. The stitches need to be placed far enough apart so that any pull on the bead doesn't tear the backing and loosen the bead(s).

What You Do

1 Stitch from the back side to the top side near the edge of the component. Approximately ½ inch (1.3 cm) over, stitch to the back side again and then up through the hole of the pendant.

2 Pick up as many beads as desired. Stitch down to the back side through the hole in the pendant.

3 Hold the bead(s) and pull the thread to adjust the tension, and then stitch up to the top side on the other side of the pendant.

4 Approximately ½ inch (1.3 cm) over, stitch to the back side again (figure 1).

5 Repeat the thread path in reverse to return to the starting place. Tie a square knot (page 14) with the needle and tail threads.

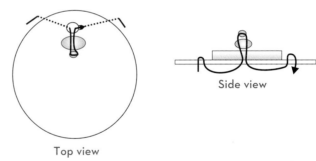

Top view

Side view

figure 1

MASK OVER THE HOLE

The hole in the pendant can also be covered by sewing on a strip of beads across the pendant over the hole, creating a mask. Or use a separate piece of bead embroidery and sew it in a place to cover the bead hole (photos, left).

USE THE HOLE

The hole can be used in a couple of different ways. One way is to hang a drop or decoration. Another is to use the hole to create a loop that can be used as a bail to string a necklace through or to attach a clasp.

What You Do

1 Complete the bead embroidery, including any edge technique selected. If using a stabilizer, be sure to cut a hole in it where the pendant hole will be.

2 Using double thread, stitch up from the back side to the top side through the backing and through the hole of the pendant. Leave a 9-inch (22.9 cm) tail.

3 Pick up enough beads to create the desired loop size.

4 Stitch back up from the back side to the top side through the backing and the bead hole (figure 2).

5 Stitch through the added beads again.

6 Repeat steps 4 and 5, if desired.

7 Use the tail and needle threads to tie a square knot (page 14). Weave the ends in and cut.

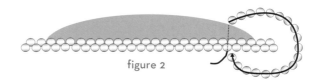

figure 2

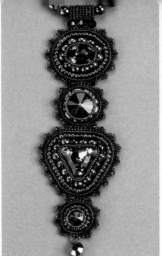

Rivolis and Crystals

A rivoli is faceted glass with a pointed back that's usually foil-backed. Similarly, crystals are cut with facets and many have a pointed or an irregular back. The shape of a rivoli or crystal presents a major challenge that's easily solved using the Create a Flat Base instructions on page 25. The base you create can cover the bottom of the component entirely or simply create a small center cradle. Once the rivoli or crystal lies steady on the backing, it can be treated just like a cabochon.

Select a bezel technique as desired for your design. The popular Plain/Standard Bezel (page 49) and Stacks Bezel (page 54) techniques are described in chapter 6. You can use those techniques with the bead sizes and counts detailed at right to fit a rivoli. You can also use other techniques, such as the Outside Window Bezel on page 50 (including twisted, page 53) or Bugle Row Bezel (page 56).

BEZEL TECHNIQUES FOR RIVOLIS FROM 12 TO 18 MM

• Plain/Standard Bezel (page 49): Create a base row using Backstitch (page 38) with size 5° or 6° seed beads (4-mm beads for 18-mm rivolis). Create a bezel row using Backstitch and size 15° seed beads.

• Stacks Bezel (page 54): For a 12-mm rivoli, use a 3-mm round or bicone bead plus two 15° seed beads. For an 18-mm rivoli, use a 4-mm round or bicone bead plus four 15° seed beads. The added beads include the turn bead (the end bead). Complete the bezel with size 15° seed beads.

BEZEL TECHNIQUES FOR RIVOLIS 20 MM AND LARGER

• Plain/Standard Bezel (page 49): Sew a base row using the Couch Stitch (page 40) with 6-mm or 8-mm round beads. Create a bezel row with size 15° or 11° beads. Or use the Outside Window Bezel (page 50) with the 6-mm or 8-mm base row.

• Stacks Bezel (page 54): Create a stack with four to six 11° seed beads. Use a bead count that covers the distance between the backing up to the edge of the rivoli. Add two more 15° beads to wrap around the rivoli's edge; the top one is the turn bead. Use 15° seed beads to complete the bezel.

Buttons

The variety of shapes, colors, and materials available today is immense. Seemingly, buttons would be very easy to use in bead embroidery because, by definition, there's the ability to sew the button to the backing. The problem with buttons arises when you wish to hide the fact that the component is, indeed, a button.

Buttons can have holes in the center, or they can have a shank on the back that lifts the button up from the surface. Each type presents unique challenges for use in bead embroidery.

STANDARD BUTTONS

First, sew the button to the backing. Bead a base row and bezel technique as desired. Now address the holes.

- Many of the techniques discussed in Pendants on page 26 can be used to hide or use the holes.

- Use the Stacks Stitch (page 37) or Loop Stitch (page 42) to add beads through the holes to create a fringelike bunch of beads to cover the holes.

- Create a separate piece of beadwork, such as a simple beaded cabochon or another design. Use the holes in the button to sew this piece down and cover the holes.

BUTTONS WITH SHANKS

The shank prevents the button from lying flat, so it would appear that the easiest solution is to cut the shank off; however, this can be dangerous if the shank

and button are both glass. Also, if the button is an antique, cutting the shank can destroy its collectible value. Cut the shank off only if it's easy and safe to do so. Then use the button just like a cabochon. If retaining the shank, do one of the following:

- If the shank is short enough, you can sew beads down and leave an empty space for the shank. After all the surrounding beads are applied, sew the button down. The bottom surface of the button will rest on the beads beneath it (figure 3).

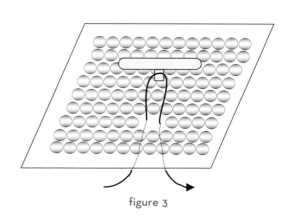

figure 3

• Follow the Create a Flat Base instructions on page 25. Then treat the button like a cabochon.

• To preserve the button's properties, create a donut base out of clay. Place the donut around the shank, and let the clay dry. Glue the donut to the backing once you're ready to use the button in your piece. Then, using a double-threaded needle, sew up through the backing, through the shank, and back down through the backing. Leave the loop on top loose. Stitch up through the backing, through the loop, and down through the backing again (figure 4). Now pull on both the needle and the tail threads to tighten the thread loops and pull the button down against the clay donut. Tie a square knot (page 14) with the needle and tail threads, weave in, and cut. The edge around the button can be covered by stitching beads around the button using Backstitch (page 38) or Couch Stitch (page 40). You can also use any of the bezel stitches in chapter 6. Or, use stacks or tall loops as illustrated in chapter 5.

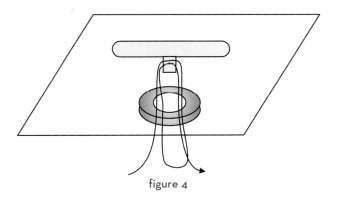

figure 4

Donuts

Donuts have large holes in the center and can be round, square, or triangular. The key, as well as the challenge, is the hole. There are several ways to deal with the donut hole using bead embroidery techniques.

COVER THE HOLE

One of the easiest and most attractive ways to deal with the donut hole is to use the hole to sew on another piece of beadwork. This has the added advantage of securing the donut to the backing while leaving an uninterrupted view of the surrounding donut surface.

What You Do

1 Create the beadwork to cover the donut hole (the beaded topper).

2 Glue the donut to the backing.

3 Use a Running Stitch (page 47) to sew through the backings of the beaded topper and through the donut hole to the backing of the larger project (figure 5).

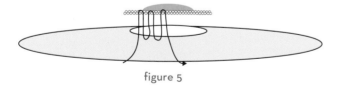

figure 5

COVER THE HOLE, ALTERNATE

Sometimes the donut hole is smaller than the area where stitches can be placed on the beaded topper, as in figure 6. In this case, you first prepare the backing that will be used for the beaded topper.

What You Do

1 Use two double-threaded needles and stitch each one through the backing of the topper before applying any beads or components onto the backing.

2 Wrap the needles and thread in a sticky note to keep them out of the way as you bead the topper.

3 Bead the topper as desired, including trimming and edging.

4 When the beaded topper is done, undo the sticky note and put needles on all the tail threads. Use the needles and threads to sew down through the donut hole into the backings (figure 6). Tie square knots, weave in, and cut.

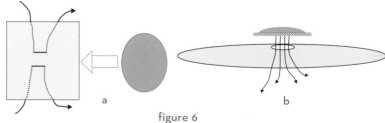

a   b

figure 6

 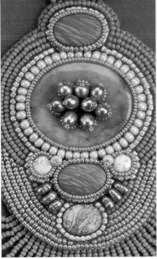  

FILL THE HOLE

Another way to deal with a donut hole is to sew beads inside it (photos above). If the hole is very small, it can often be filled by sewing one bead. Or use the Stacks Stitch (page 37), Picot Stitch (page 41), or Loop Stitch (page 42) to add beads inside the hole.

KEEP THE HOLE

You can use the hole as part of your design (photos below).

What You Do

1 During the preparation process, place the donut on the backing. Use a fine-tip pen to trace the donut hole onto the backing.

2 Cut the donut center out of the backing and then place the donut on the backing again and test the hole cut. Trim as needed.

3 Glue the donut down and sew the beads on. Use any bezel technique to hold the donut to the backing like you would with a cabochon.

4 When you're ready to attach the outer-backing, again place the piece on the outer-backing, trace the hole, and then cut. Trim as needed and then glue the outer-backing on.

5 From the back side, use Whipstitch (page 47) to sew the outer-backing to the backing at the center of the hole.

Other Objects

This section includes everything from shells, mineral specimens, or stone slices to whatever you want to use that's not a bead. There are many objects with interesting textures and colors that can spark your imagination. The key to using these other objects effectively is first to identify the beading challenge presented by them.

- If the bottom isn't flat, see Create a Flat Base on page 25.

- If the edge is thin with a hollow center (like many shells or metal stampings), fill in the center with clay.

- Use the various bezel techniques in chapter 6 to secure the component to the backing.

- Use tall stacks (page 37) and/or tall loops (page 42) to hide any unwanted rough edges.

Last Words on Components

- Think creatively!

- Sew objects on top of objects, beadwork on top of beadwork.

- Make separate bead-embroidered pieces and combine them into one.

- Create your own component: use a glass form (available at craft stores) and glue a favorite picture to the back to create your own cabochon.

CHAPTER 5

Surface Stitches

The mainstay of bead embroidery is found in the stitches that apply beads to the surface of a backing. You can completely cover the surface or add beads in strategic places to create a design.

A Few Rules for Stitches

- Use single thread, except where indicated.

- Pull the thread firmly so the beads are secure; however, do not pull so tightly that you bend, twist, or torque the backing. In other words, keep the surface of the backing flat.

- Use a thread length that's easy to work with. While 2 yards (1.8 m) is good as a general rule, it can differ from one beader to another. Adding a new thread in bead embroidery isn't as cumbersome as many other beading techniques, so use what's comfortable for you. As a general rule, start a new thread by doing three Whipstitch loops (page 47) and a half-hitch knot (page 15). End a thread with a half-hitch knot and then three Whipstitch loops.

When you're starting out with a project, you may struggle with stitch/bead placement, trying to be precise with the stitching. However, you'll find that as the beads fill the surface, the placement of any individual bead is affected by the beads that surround it. Rows become smoother because of the surrounding rows. Beads get "nudged" into place by the beads next to them. So relax and enjoy the synergies of bead embroidery.

One-Bead Stitch

The easiest application of bead embroidery is stitching on one bead. Although simple, this can be a very effective technique to decorate a surface, especially when you use beads of various shapes and sizes.

WHAT YOU DO

1 Determine the bead's position with the bead hole parallel to the backing.

2 Stitch up to the top side just under one of the bead holes.

3 Stitch through the bead and down to the back side just under the other bead hole.

4 Repeat steps 2 and 3. For beads larger than 4 mm or size 5° seed, repeat again (figure 1).

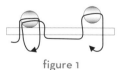

figure 1

5 If the bead is large and curved, stitch through the backing next to where the bead touches the surface, instead of under the bead holes. This will allow the thread to be pulled tightly without altering the flatness of the backing (figure 2).

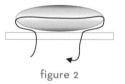

figure 2

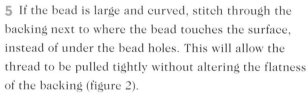

tip | When the exact position of the bead is important, use a small dab of thick, sticky glue that dries quickly to position the bead before stitching.

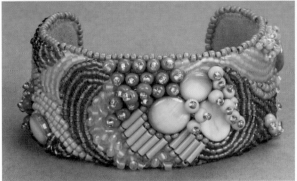

Stacks Stitch (a.k.a. Fringe Stitch)

When you stitch on one bead, the hole is parallel to the surface, but with the Stacks Stitch, the hole is perpendicular to the surface. Turning the bead this way provides a very different appearance and texture. You can easily add bulk and change the height of the surface with this stitch, which is performed just like regular fringe that hangs from an edge but is stitched onto a backing. Like fringe, there's a bead (or beads) and a turn bead.

WHAT YOU DO

1 Pick up the stack bead(s) plus one more bead (usually an 11° seed bead), referred to as a turn bead.

2 Move all the beads down to the surface of the backing.

3 Skip the last bead added (the turn bead) and stitch back through the stack bead(s) and through the backing to the underside. Hold the turn bead with one hand and the thread with the other and pull to adjust the tension (figure 3).

4 Stitch up to the top side in the next placement area and repeat.

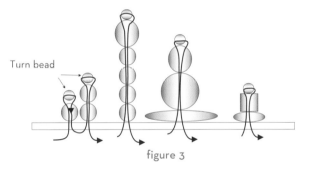

figure 3

Stacks with Many Beads

Stacks may be stitched with many beads; however, the increased weight needs to be considered as you stitch. Stacks can be stressed or pulled due to the nature of the beaded item. For instance, a beaded eyeglass case inside a purse will get rubbed or tossed around. One way to provide an adequate base area between the Stack Stitches is, instead of stitching one stack over, skip two or more stacks over so that the area of the material being stitched on is wider and therefore stronger (shown in sample A). Sample B shows what not to do: there's very little material between the Stack Stitches, and if a stack is pulled firmly, that small area could tear.

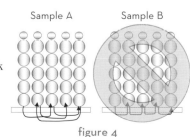

figure 4

Backstitch

One of the most widely used stitches in bead embroidery, Backstitch is used to cover a surface in a row of beads while creating a pattern, providing texture, or painting a picture. Typically, it's done with 11° seed beads, but it's also a great stitch to use with smaller beads like 15° seeds or larger beads like 5° seeds. Other kinds of beads can also be used effectively as long as the desired result is a row of beads. So, 4-mm round beads or even 8-mm bicone beads are possible choices for this stitch.

There are many variations of Backstitch. For example, 1-1 Backstitch, 2-3 Backstitch, 4-2 Backstitch, and 4-6 Backstitch are all common variations. Each can be used whenever a Backstitch process is called for; choose whichever variation you feel most comfortable with or most proficient in using. All of the variations use the same process.

> **tip**
> I like the 4-6 Backstitch because it covers areas faster and has a smoother line than the other variations. However, when beading a tight curve or corner, switch to a 2-3 Backstitch. You can switch the bead count (and back again) within a beaded row as desired.

WHAT YOU DO

1 Pick up the count of beads in the first number (so if you're working with a 2-3 backstitch, pick up two beads) and stitch down into the backing.

2 From the back side, count backward (including the added beads) and stitch up to the top side. When counting backward, use the count of the second number in the name of the stitch.

3 Stitch through the bead holes again. The number of beads being stitched through will equal the second number in the name of the stitch you are using.

4 Repeat until you've completed the row.

2-3 Backstitch

Pick up two beads and stitch down (figure 5a). Count backward three and stitch up. Stitch through the three beads (figure 5b).

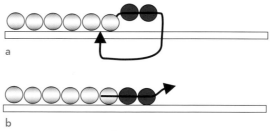

figure 5

4-2 Backstitch

Pick up four beads and stitch down (figure 6a). Count backward two and stitch up. Stitch through the two beads (figure 6b).

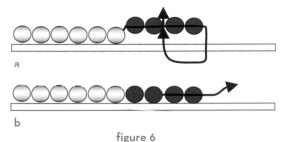

figure 6

4-6 Backstitch

Pick up four beads and stitch down (figure 7a). Count backward six and stitch up. Stitch through all six beads (figure 7b).

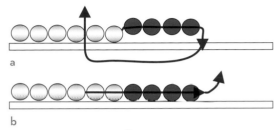

figure 7

Backstitch Tips

• When adding beads, be sure to leave plenty of room for the added beads as you stitch forward. If you stitch too close, the added beads will bow upward. If you stitch too far ahead, it's not a problem because the beads can be pushed back into proper position and anchored on the backward part of the stitch.

• As you stitch through the beads, the friction of the needle and thread will pull the beads in the same direction and create spaces between the beads in the row. Use your fingers to push the beads back into position before stitching through the backing. Pulling the thread tight isn't going to create a close fit. It's the positioning of the beads that creates a close-fitting, smooth row.

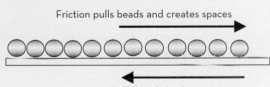

Friction pulls beads and creates spaces

Push beads back into position

• When stitching multiple rows of Backstitch, whether in a straight line or a curve, it's usually easier to stitch in one direction than the other. So, instead of stitching back and forth to create the rows, stitch in one direction only. Once you've stitched the bead line, return to the top side and stitch through the bead holes to travel back to the starting spot. Be careful not to pull

the thread too tightly and pull the beads out of place. Stitch down into the back side, and then up, positioning the needle to create the next row. This process also straightens the beads. So if you're stitching a row of Backstitch that's not surrounded by any other beads, consider stitching through the holes multiple times. This will fill up the holes in the beads with thread and line up the beads more evenly.

• The Backstitch is not only the most widely used stitch in bead embroidery, but it's also one of the most versatile. You can create straight or curved rows using many sizes of beads. You can also Backstitch on top of rows already stitched to add even more texture (see below).

Couch Stitch

This stitch creates a row of beads just like Backstitch does, but the Couch Stitch process allows you to fit an entire row of beads from one point to another in one step, and then go back and anchor the beads down. Although this can be used for all sizes of beads, it's particularly useful for large beads (4 mm and up). It's also necessary when using beads that are uniform in size but need to fit in a specific space. Because you pick up all the beads at once, you can adjust and fit the beads into a space more effectively than you can using Backstitch.

WHAT YOU DO

1 Pick up the desired number of beads and stitch down into the backing in a forward direction. This creates the bead row (figure 8).

2 Anchor the beads by stitching up through the backing at the intersection of the nearest two beads. Loop over the thread between the beads and stitch back down into the backing. Pull until the loop is just above the thread line and hidden between the beads. Don't

> **tip** Use the anchor stitch as described in step 2 to push or pull a row of beads into a desired position. So, use it on a row of Backstitch (page 38) or Lazy Stitch (page 43) to nudge the beads to a desired spot.

pull so tightly that the row created in step 1 is pulled down onto the backing.

3 Repeat the loops/anchoring process in step 2 to the end of the row and then back to the beginning (figure 9).

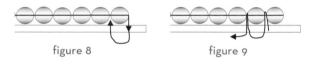

figure 8   figure 9

> **tip** If you're stitching a long length of Couch Stitch or stitching one or more curves, it's easier if you place anchors at several key spots to hold the shape of the row before stitching between each bead. So do the anchor stitch as described in step 2, except skip as many beads in the row as needed to get to the next key spot. Then go back and anchor between each bead.

Two-Needle Couch Stitch Variation

A common variation of the Couch Stitch is the Two-Needle Couch Stitch, typically used when the beads are 6 mm or larger. This process will provide more strength and stability for those larger beads. Create the row with one of the needles using double thread. Use the second needle with single thread to anchor the row (figure 10).

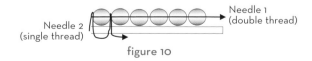

Needle 2
(single thread)
                    Needle 1
                    (double thread)

figure 10

Picot Stitch (a.k.a. Moss Stitch)

This stitch creates a fabulous texture that feels like a nubby carpet of beads. It's easy to use as a fill-in for areas both large and small and is useful for filling in small, irregular-shaped areas on the backing where you want some bulk and/or texture. Any size beads can be used, and you can mix the bead sizes even within the stitch. Beads larger than 8° seed beads will need double thread to accommodate the added weight. Colors can be monochromatic or as varied as you want.

WHAT YOU DO

1 Stitch up to the top side from the back side. Pick up three beads, then move the beads down to the backing and stitch down near the first added bead. Pull until the middle bead rests on top of the other two beads (figure 11).

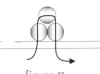

figure 11

2 Repeat step 1 as desired.

The first and third beads are the base beads and the center bead is the topper. For a more random appearance, outline the area to be covered, alternating the direction of the picot as shown in figure 12. Repeat around the entire border of the area to be covered.

Then, fill in the center with picots, changing directions: horizontal, vertical, and on a slant for a random appearance.

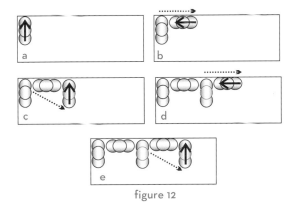

figure 12

tip

When filling in, if there's an area where only one bead will fit, stitch up to the top through one of the base beads of one of the previous picots. Pick up two beads and stitch down into the area to fill. If there's an area to fill in that won't accommodate any base beads, stitch up through the base bead of a previous picot, pick up one bead, and stitch down through the base bead of another previous picot.

Loop Stitch

The Loop Stitch is a variation of the picot. Use it to add texture and a free-flowing feeling to the beaded surface. As with the picot, colors can be monochromatic or as varied as you want. You can also experiment with bead sizes to create a unique surface. The stitch is executed just like the Picot Stitch (page 41), except you use more than three beads. Generally, single thread is used; however, if using beads larger than 11° seed beads or if the loop is particularly tall, either use double thread or stitch through the loop twice.

tip

Loops have more beads and are therefore heavier than a Picot Stitch. Also, because the loops are raised from the surface, there's a greater chance they'll get pulled. In step 4, the stitching is positioned to provide a greater area on the backing material so there's more stability and less chance of tearing.

WHAT YOU DO

1 Stitch up from the back side to the top side.

2 Pick up the desired number of beads.

3 Move the beads down the thread to the backing and stitch down near the first added bead.

4 For the next loop, stitch two beads forward from the previous loop to start, as shown in figure 13.

5 Repeat steps 1 through 4 as needed.

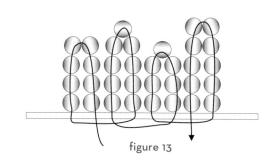

figure 13

Lazy Stitch

This stitch covers an area with beads quickly, which is probably how it got its name. The Lazy Stitch is useful in creating color and texture patterns. Use it to create short rows of beads that are next to each other. Line up the rows or create diagonals or a checkerboard. The possibilities are endless!

WHAT YOU DO

1 Stitch up from the back side at the top of the row.

2 Pick up the desired number of beads (usually from three to seven).

3 Stitch down into the backing, leaving space for the beads at the bottom of the row.

4 To add the next row, stitch up to the top side again at the top of the row (figure 14).

5 Repeat steps 2 through 4 as desired.

Top view

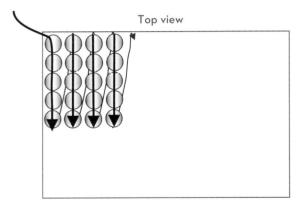

Side view

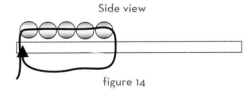

figure 14

tip Use double thread for bead sizes larger than an 11° seed bead, or stitch through the beads twice or more.

Chain-o-Beads Stitch

This is made of seed beads combined with a larger bead for the fill bead. The instructions below are for 11° seed beads and a fill bead that's 4 mm. Adjust the bead count and needle placement to use other bead sizes; the stitch path will be the same.

WHAT YOU DO

1 Draw a line on the backing to define the center of the row you're creating.

2 Stitch up to the top side through the centerline, one seed bead width down from the top.

3 Pick up one fill bead. Stitch down into the backing, forward on the centerline (figure 15a).

4 Stitch up from the back side at the top to the left of the line. Pick up two seed beads and stitch down through to the back side. Position the needle so the length is two seed beads long and around the fill bead (figure 15b). (Two beads is approximately one-half the length of a 4-mm fill bead. Adjust the bead count as needed for other fill bead sizes.)

5 Repeat step 4, but stitch to the right instead of the left (figure 15c).

6 Stitch up from the back side at the top and to the left of the line. Stitch through the two beads added previously. Pick up three or four seed beads as needed to encircle the fill bead. Push the fill bead with one hand so it rests firmly at the top. Stitch down through the backing to the left of the line at the bottom (figure 15d).

7 Repeat step 6 but stitch to the right instead of the left (figure 15e).

8 Stitch up through the backing at the top of the fill bead. Stitch through the fill bead and down through the backing at the bottom of the fill bead (figure 15f).

9 Repeat steps 2 through 8 for the length desired.

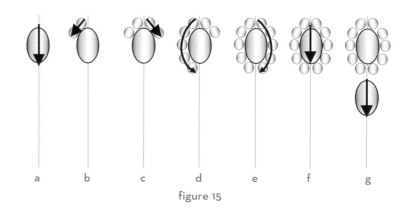

figure 15

Clover Stitch

This stitch is named for the three-leaf clover it resembles. Use it to add texture or flowerlike patterns to the beadwork. Use bead sizes from 4 to 8 mm and shapes from round to oval and even flat round (a.k.a. coin) to flat oval (a.k.a. puffed oval).

WHAT YOU DO

1 Set the beads down on the backing where you want them to be placed and find the center point. Mark the center point and remove the beads.

2 Mark three outside circle points measuring out from the center point using the bead size, spreading equally around the circle (i.e., if using a 6-mm bead, mark out from the center 6 mm).

3 Stitch up from the back side through one of the outside points.

4 Pick up one 6-mm bead and stitch down to the back side in the center of the circle.

5 Stitch up to the top side through the next point on the outside of the circle. Repeat step 4.

tip Substitute the 6-mm bead with a 4- or an 8-mm bead, and use the instructions above to create different-size clovers.

6 Repeat step 5 for the last bead (figure 16).

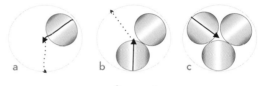

figure 16

7 Stitch up to the top side through the first outside circle point (where the first 6-mm bead was added). Repeat steps 4 through 6. In other words, reinforce your work by repeating the thread path for all three beads.

8 Stitch up to the top side at the outside of the circle where the first 6-mm bead was added. Stitch through that bead and pick up one 11° seed bead. Stitch out through the second added 6-mm bead and then down into the backing (figure 17a).

9 Stitch up to the top side at the outside of the circle where the last 6-mm bead was added. Stitch through that bead and the 11° seed bead. Stitch out through the first added 6-mm bead and then down into the backing (figure 17b).

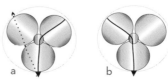

figure 17

Braid Stitch

This stitch adds a twist and turn to the surface, like a braid. It's used to cover a surface or provide an interesting border on surfaces not covered entirely with beads.

WHAT YOU DO

1 Draw a line on the backing that indicates the center of the braid.

2 Stitch up to the top side to the left of the line, so that one bead will fit completely to the left of the line—touching it, but not on it.

3 Pick up seven seed beads.

4 Position the needle forward the length of six beads. Because we're using seven beads but a length of only six beads, it will make the beads bow, creating a slight loop above the backing. Position the needle on the opposite side of the line so the bead is touching the line (on the *other* side of the line, not the side the stitch started on). Stitch down through the backing.

5 Stitch up to the top side, in a backward direction, halfway up the previous loop stitched. Stay on the same side of the line.

6 Repeat steps 3 through 5 until you have the desired length (figure 18).

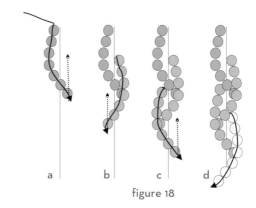

a   b   c   d

figure 18

Other Stitches

The stitches in this section are used in bead embroidery, although not to add beads. Instead, these are primarily employed in the construction process rather than the bead decoration process.

Running Stitch

The Running Stitch is a simple stitch used to "travel" from one place to another on the beadwork. Stitch straight up and down all the way through the backing in small increments. Be careful to stay between the beads and not interfere with the beadwork (figure 19).

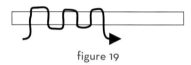

figure 19

Whipstitch

This stitch can be used to sew two pieces of fabric and/or backing together. To sew two pieces together, stitch near the edge through both pieces. Loop the thread around the edges and stitch again as illustrated in figure 20.

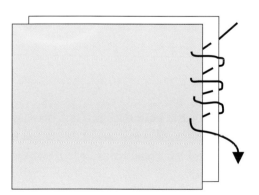

figure 20

You can also use this stitch when your needle and thread end up in one area but need to start the next phase in another area. From the back side of the beadwork, stitch through the backing, approximately ½ inch (1.3 cm) wide. As you stitch through the backing, be careful not to interfere with the beadwork on the top side. Move a short space nearer to your destination and repeat (figure 21). Continue until you end up at the spot you need to be. This stitch is also perfect for weaving in threads after a knot.

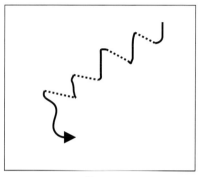

figure 21

tip

To secure the thread tension, use a half-hitch knot (page 15) before traveling and then end with another half-hitch knot.

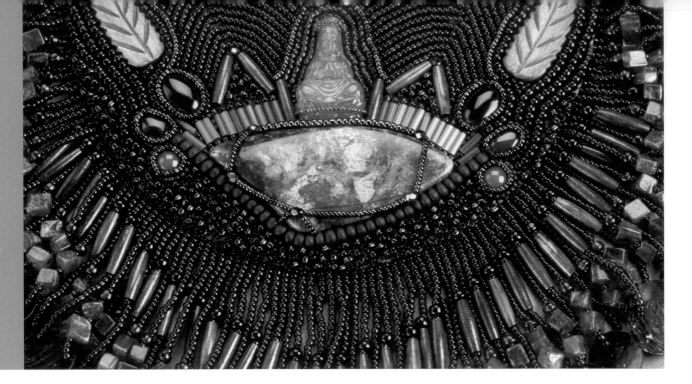

CHAPTER 6

Bezel Stitches

The best way to make sure a component doesn't come off is to encase it. In other words, create a bezel with beads that will hold the component on the backing. But bezels aren't just practical; they also offer a great decorative technique. So, even when the center of your project is a bead or a button that doesn't require a bezel, you may still want one to add design features and integrate the component into the rest of the design.

Getting Started

First glue the component onto the backing *and* sew it on if using a bead or button. Use a good, strong glue (see pages 13 and 24 for more about gluing components to your projects) to hold the component in place while the bezel beads are sewn on. Once the bezel is sewn on, the beadwork will help hold the component in place.

The bezel stitches described in this chapter use single thread unless otherwise noted. Use a comfortable length of thread, usually 2 yards (1.8 m), and add thread as needed.

Plain/Standard Bezel

This is the simplest bezel in terms of design and is therefore perfect for patterned or fancy components where you just wish to frame the component. In practical terms, this can be used for any domed component where the edge has an upward slant toward the center. Accordingly, this stitch is perfect for cabochons. The Plain Bezel is also great for other edge shapes (squared or curved) where the bezel row can be placed so that it's inside the outer edge of the component. This is usually achieved by first creating a base row of large beads, so that when you add the bezel row inside the base row, it's lifted up over the edge of the component. This technique is referred to as a Bead Raised Bezel.

WHAT YOU DO

1 The first row you'll bead will actually be the second row from the center of the component—the base row. Use either a Backstitch (page 38) or Couch Stitch (page 40). Select a bead size that will lift the inside row of beads above the edge. Stitch as close as possible to the edge of the component.

2 Once you complete the base row, stitch through the row (around through the holes only) three or more

times. This strengthens the row and straightens the beads by filling up the bead holes. Then stitch to the back side and tie a knot. You can continue the next steps using the same thread, or weave in and cut this thread if you wish to change thread colors.

3 Using a Backstitch (page 38), stitch a row of beads between the component and the base row. Generally, the bead size for the bezel row is smaller than the size used for the base row; however, this isn't an absolute rule. Use any size you like to accomplish your design objectives. This key row that holds the component to the backing is called the *bezel row*.

4 Once the row is complete, stitch through the row (around through the holes only) three or more times to strengthen it and straighten the beads by filling up the bead holes. Then stitch to the back side, tie a knot, weave in the ends, and cut.

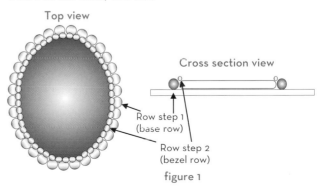

figure 1

Outside Window Bezel

If the component is tall, you may choose to include a row of large beads (5 mm and bigger) around it. The large beads will hide the edge and/or blend the tall component into the piece. When using large beads, there are often gaps between the beads, especially when using round or bicone-shaped beads. A great design choice is to use this Outside Window Bezel because it will fill in those gaps while also creating the bezel.

WHAT YOU DO

1 Refer to figure 2 for steps 1 to 4. Using a Backstitch (page 38) or Couch Stitch (page 40), stitch your base row of beads around the component. Select any bead size desired.

2 Using single thread, stitch up from the back side to the top side in the spaces between the beads on the base row as illustrated. Leave a 9-inch (22.9 cm) tail.

3 Refer to the Stacks Stitch (page 37). To create your first stack around the base row, pick up seed beads plus

one turn bead. You can select seed beads of various sizes (from 15° to 6°). The size used for the stack (typically 11°) doesn't have to be the same size (or color) as the turn bead (which is typically 15°). For the turn bead, use the bead you've chosen for the bezel row. Use a bead count that will place the bezel row in the desired area around the component.

4 Skip the turn bead and stitch back through the added beads and backing. Hold the turn bead with one hand and pull on the thread with the other hand to adjust the tension. Be careful not to pull too tightly. The stack should be loose enough to comfortably bend around the base row and lie flat against the component. Stitch from the back side to the top side in the next space between base row beads.

figure 2

5 Repeat steps 3 and 4 around the component, ending on the back side. Use the tail and needle threads to tie a square knot (page 14). Weave in the ends and cut.

6 Using doubled thread, create the bezel row. Add a stop bead (page 14) and leave a 9-inch (22.9 cm) tail.

7 Stitch through the turn bead at the top of one of the stacks. Pick up beads that are the same size as the turn bead of the stack, and use a bead count that spans the length to the next stack. Stitch through the turn bead of the next stack (figure 3). Repeat to return to the starting position. The bead count added between stacks may not be the same around the component. For example, the straighter sides of a component may require more beads than a curved area or corner. Adjust the counts as needed.

8 Stitch through the bezel row beads over to the next stack. Remove the stop bead. Pull the tail and needle threads to adjust the tension. Look at the bezel row. It should lie tight and flat next to the component. If it's loose, there are too many beads. If there are gaps between the beads, you didn't add enough beads. To fix this, pull the thread, remove the beads, and start over at step 7, but adjust the bead counts used. When you're satisfied, continue with the next step.

9 Repeat the thread path around the bezel row to strengthen and straighten the beads. Repeat as often as needed. With the needle thread, stitch down through a stack to the back side. Put a needle on each tail thread and stitch down the stack to the back side (figure 4). Tie a square knot with the threads. Weave in the ends and cut.

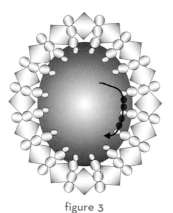

figure 3

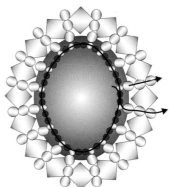

figure 4

Twisted Bezel

This bezel makes a fabulous design "twist" and is therefore perfect for adding visual spice to monochromatic components. Because the twisted center of the bezel is done with Stacks Stitch (page 37), you can easily manipulate the position of the twisted row. This ability to place the twist on the edge or deeply in toward the center of the component is very useful.

WHAT YOU DO

1 Use a Backstitch (page 38) or Couch Stitch (page 40) to stitch the base row.

2 Using single thread, stitch up from the back side to the top side between the component and the base row. Leave a 9-inch (22.9 cm) tail. Stitch through two beads of the base row.

3 Refer to the Stacks Stitch (page 37). To create stacks around the component, pick up seed beads plus one

turn bead. This looks great with size 11° beads for the stack and a size 15° bead for the turn bead. Use a bead count for the stack that will place the twist in the desired area. So for a twist close to the edge, use one bead. For a twist that's closer to the center, use as many as needed. Skip the turn bead and stitch back through the added beads plus some beads in the base row—use a count in the base row that will give you the spacing you want. Closer spacing results in tighter twists; longer spacing results in loose, sleek ones. Hold the turn bead with one hand and pull on the thread with the other hand to adjust the tension, being careful not to pull too tightly. The fringe should be loose and lie flat comfortably against the component. Repeat all around the component, and then stitch down to the back side (figure 5).

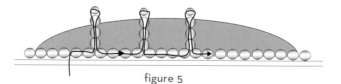

figure 5

4 If desired, you can strengthen and straighten the base row. Stitch over two bead lengths and then up to the top side. Stitch around the base row through the bead holes only, several times. Stitch down to the back side. Tie a square knot (page 14) with the tail and needle threads. Weave in the ends and cut.

5 Use doubled thread to create the twists. Add a stop bead with a 9-inch (22.9 cm) tail. Stitch through the turn bead at the top of one of the stacks.

6 Pick up beads that are the same size that were used for the turn bead of the stack. Skip the next stack and stitch through the turn bead two stacks over as illustrated (figure 6). Use a bead count that provides for a very slight loop over the skipped stack. Repeat around the component.

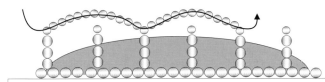

figure 6

To create an Outside Window Twisted Bezel, complete steps 1 through 5 for the Outside Window Bezel (page 50). Then do steps 5 through 9 for the Twisted Bezel (page 52).

7 If there's an even number of stacks, you'll return to the starting stack. Stitch down into the stack beads and through the backing to the back side. Stitch up from the back side to the top side and through the beads of the next stack. If there are an odd number of stacks, you'll be able to continue without stitching through the backings. Repeat around the component for a second time, except you'll need to go under the loop already there before stitching through the next stack turn bead (figure 7).

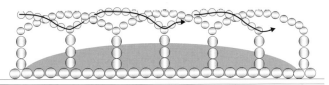

figure 7

8 Stitch one more stack over. Remove the stop bead and pull on both ends to adjust the tension. If the twist is too tight and there are gaps between beads of the twist, remove the beads and start over at step 5 using more beads. If the twist is too loose, remove the beads and start over at step 5 using fewer beads. Although you may resist starting over, removing the beads is fairly quick and easy!

9 When you have the tension correct on the twist, stitch down to the back side, through the stack beads with each of the thread ends. Tie knots, weave in, and cut.

Stacks Bezel

Tall or irregular edges on a component present a challenge that's easily dealt with using a Stacks Bezel. This bezel can also be used to add a design element by including various shaped beads to the stacks. Unlike the other bezels so far, this one is created without a base row. You can place the stacks next to each other to create a wall of beads that hide the side edge of the component. Or, place stacks far apart, leaving windows that display the side of the component.

WHAT YOU DO

1 Using single thread, add a stop bead with a 9-inch (22.9 cm) tail. Stitch up from the back side to the top side near the outer edge of the component. If the edge of the component is above the backing, it's helpful to draw a line on the backing where the stacks will be placed (refer to the bottom photo on page 29).

2 Referring to the Stacks Stitch (page 37), pick up beads for the stack, plus a turn bead. Make sure the stack is high enough that the turn bead sits above the edge of the component. (The number of beads used for each stack can change around components that have high edges in one area and lower edges in others.) Skip the turn bead and stitch back through the other beads in the stack and through the backing. Hold the turn bead with one hand and pull the thread with the other hand to adjust the tension. Don't pull too tightly. Check to make sure the stack will bend and form around the component edge.

3 Repeat step 2 around the component. If you're using narrow stacks around the component, such as a stack of seeds or bugles, stitch every other stack around the component (figure 8). Then circle again, filling in the blank spaces (figure 9). This provides more stability by creating a larger area of backing between stitches.

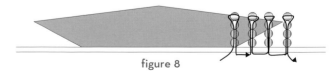

figure 8

Even from the side, Stacks Bezels are wow!

figure 9

4 Finish near the tail thread. Remove the stop bead and use the tail and needle threads to tie a square knot (page 14). Weave the ends in and cut.

5 Use doubled thread for the next steps. Add a stop bead with a 9-inch (22.9 cm) tail. Stitch through one of the turn beads. Add beads as needed to span between the current turn bead and the next. Continue around the component to return to the beginning.

6 Remove the stop bead and pull on the tail and needle threads to test the tension. If the row has gaps, you didn't add enough beads. If the row is too loose or buckles, you added too many beads. To fix, pull the thread, remove the beads, and start over at step 5, but adjust the bead counts. When you're satisfied, continue with the next step.

7 Stitch around the bezel row again and stitch down through a stack to the back side. Put needles on the tail threads. Stitch each down through a stack to the back side. Use the tail and needle threads to tie a square knot. Weave the ends in and cut.

tip

If you want close, evenly spaced stacks that hide edges (such as those of rivolis), use the Square Stitch (page 82) to create a woven strip to use as the stacks. Then stitch the woven strip to the backing, adding the turn bead as it's stitched.

Other Options

Combine other types of beads with the seed beads in the stack.

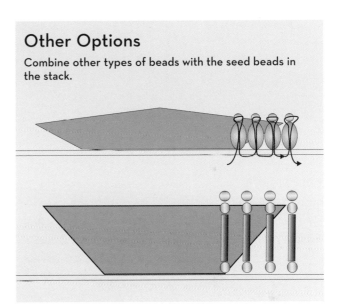

Bugle Row Bezel

You can use this technique to place the bezel row far up toward the center of the component to create a fabulous line of beads. Because the bugle row is wide, it's a great technique for covering imperfections in the component—such as cracks, breaks, or scratches—or to cover drill holes on pendants. This is also useful for irregularly shaped components, because you can decide where to place the bugle rows. Even though the bugle rows are wide, strategic placement allows for a large window between the rows so that much of the surface of the component remains visible. One of the main benefits of this bezel is it easily accommodates a very thick component.

WHAT YOU DO

1 If desired, create a base row around the component using a Backstitch (page 38) or Couch Stitch (page 40). A base row isn't necessary for this bezel and is strictly a design choice.

2 Decide where you want to stitch the bugle rows. Using single thread, add a stop bead with a 9-inch (22.9) tail.

3 Stitch up from the back side to the top side next to the component. If a base row was created, stitch between the base row and the component. Position the needle at one end of the intended bugle row.

4 Pick up one seed, one bugle, and one seed. Stitch down to the back side at the other end of the intended bugle row. Pull the thread so the beads rest above the base row (if created). Don't pull so tightly that the base row pulls away from the edge of the component. If there's no base row, pull so the row of seed-bugle-seed rests on the backing. Stitch up to the top side at the original spot in step 3. Stitch through the seed-bugle-seed again (figure 10).

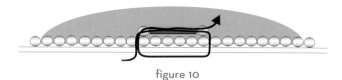

figure 10

5 Pick up one seed, one bugle, and one seed. Stitch through the previous seed-bugle-seed and back through the added seed-bugle-seed (figure 11). Repeat until you have the desired bugle row length (figure 12).

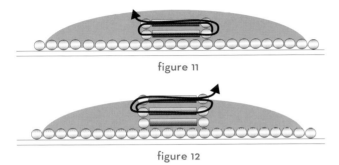

figure 11

figure 12

6 Stitch back to the edge, weaving back and forth through the seed-bugle-seed rows until you reach the first row (figure 13). Stitch to the back side.

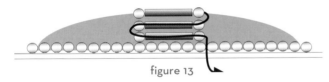

figure 13

7 Repeat steps 3 through 6 until you have all the bugle rows stitched. Remove the stop bead and use the tail and needle threads to tie a square knot (page 14). Weave the ends in and cut.

8 Use single thread for the bezel row. Add a stop bead with a 9-inch (22.9 cm) tail.

9 Stitch through the top seed-bugle-seed of one of the bugle rows. Pick up enough seed beads to span the distance between two bugle rows. Repeat around to return to where you started.

10 Remove the stop bead and pull the tail and needle threads to adjust the tension (figure 14). If the row is too tight or there are gaps, you didn't add enough beads; on the other hand, if the row is too loose and buckles, you added too many beads. To fix, pull the thread, remove the beads, and start over at step 9. When you're satisfied, continue with the next step.

figure 14

11 Put a needle on the tail thread and weave down the bugle row to the back side (as done in figure 13). With the original needle thread, stitch back through the bezel row (around through the holes only) several times to strengthen the bezel row and make the beads in the row line up. Finally, weave down one of the bugle rows and stitch to the back side (again, like in figure 13). With each thread end, tie a knot, weave in, and cut.

Bead-Across Bezel

The Bead-Across Bezel uses a larger decorative bead sewn to the backing in selected places, usually on top of a base row. You then add smaller beads between these larger beads to create a varied and unique bezel row. This technique is particularly useful with components that are flat on top, have corners, or have an irregular shape. This bezel adds a wonderful decoration while holding the component in place.

WHAT YOU DO

1 If desired, create a base row around the component using a Backstitch (page 38) or Couch Stitch (page 40). A base row isn't necessary for this bezel and is strictly a design choice.

2 Decide where you want to stitch the larger beads. Use a 3-mm bead, a size 8° seed bead, or a larger bead, as desired.

3 Using single thread, stitch up from the back side to the top side next to the component where you want the bead to be placed. If there's a base row, stitch between the component and the base row. Pick up the bead and stitch down to the back side. If there's a base row, stitch between the component and the base row. Pull the thread to adjust the tension so the bead sits on top of the base row or backing. Repeat the stitch path again (figure 15). Repeat the stitch path one more time (for a total of three times) and stitch over to the area for the next bead (figure 16).

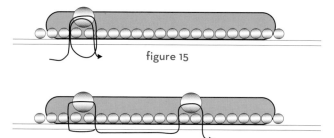

figure 15

figure 16

4 Repeat step 3 until all beads are placed. Then stitch over to the first bead attached and stitch up and through the bead one more time, then down to the back side. Use the tail and needle threads to tie a square knot (page 14). Weave the ends in and cut.

5 Using doubled thread, add a stop bead with a 9-inch (22.9 cm) tail.

6 Stitch through one of the added beads. Pick up beads (usually size 15° seed beads) to span the distance to the next attached bead. Repeat until you return to where you started (figure 17).

figure 17

7 Remove the stop bead and pull the tail and needle threads to adjust the tension. You didn't add enough beads if there are gaps between the beads, or if the attached beads are being pulled up too far from the base row. If the bezel is too loose or buckles, then you added too many beads. To fix this, pull the thread, remove the beads, and start over at step 6, but adjust the bead counts used. When you're satisfied, continue with the next step.

8 Add a needle to each of the tail threads. Stitch down to the back side. If there's a base row, stitch between the component and base row.

9 With the needle thread, stitch around the bezel row one more time (more if desired). End at the starting point. Stitch down to the back side. If there's a base row, stitch between the component and base row. Use the tail and needle threads to tie a square knot. Weave the ends in and cut.

Use Combinations
You can combine bezel techniques to solve edge problems and to achieve fantastic design results.

Flower Bezel

Here's a perfect example of a bezel that adds a design aspect while holding a component. Apply it completely around the component, or bead bits of it strategically to create a unique design. You can also use this bezel to hide imperfections in the component—scratches, spots, or cracks, for example—or a hole drilled in a pendant. In the instructions below, the base row and flower beads are 11° seed beads; however, you can change the bead sizes for a variety of effects.

WHAT YOU DO

1 Using a Backstitch (page 38) or Couch Stitch (page 40), stitch a base row around the component.

2 Using single thread, stitch up from the back side to the top side between the component and the base row. Leave a 9-inch (22.9 cm) tail.

3 Stitch through beads of the base row and stitch down to the back side. Use a count of beads in the base row that's equal to two of the beads that will be used for

the flower. For example, if the base row uses 11° seeds and the flower is created with 11° seeds, stitch through two base row beads. If the base row is a 4-mm bead, and the flower is 11° seeds, stitch through one base row bead. Stitch up to the top side and through the bead(s) in the base row again (figure 18).

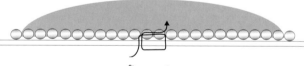

figure 18

4 Pick up two seed beads. Stitch through the beads in the base row and then the added beads again (figure 19).

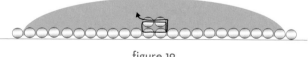

figure 19

5 Pick up six 11° seed beads. Stitch through the first of the two beads added in step 4. Pick up one 8° or one

11° seed bead, which will be the center of the flower, and stitch through the third added bead (figure 20).

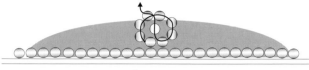

figure 20

6 Pick up two 15° seed beads; they will be the bezel row beads. Stitch back through the two seed beads below and around the flower to return to the starting spot (figure 21).

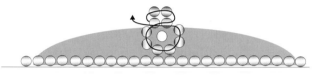

figure 21

7 Stitch up through the two bezel row beads again and down through the first of the beads below. Stitch through the flower center bead and one of the flower beads on the bottom. Stitch through the base row beads again (figure 22).

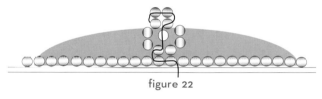

figure 22

8 Stitch over to the next area where you want a flower. Repeat steps 3 through 7 until you have all the flowers you want. Stitch to the back side. Use the needle thread and tail threads to tie a square knot (page 14). Weave the ends in and cut.

9 Using single thread, add a stop bead with a 9-inch (22.9 cm) tail.

10 Stitch through the top two beads of one flower. Pick up beads, using a bead count that will span the distance to the next flower. Repeat until you return to the start (figure 23).

figure 23

11 Remove the stop bead and pull the tail and needle threads to adjust the tension. If gaps show between the beads, or the flowers are being pulled up too far from the base row, you didn't add enough beads. Conversely, too many beads were added if the bezel is too loose or if it buckles. To fix, pull the thread, remove the beads, and start over at step 10, but adjust the bead counts used. When you feel satisfied with the results, continue with the next step.

12 Put a needle on the tail thread. Weave down through the flower to the back side. With the needle thread, repeat the path around the bezel row two or more times. Weave down through the flower to the back side. Use the tail and needle threads to tie a square knot. Weave the ends in and cut.

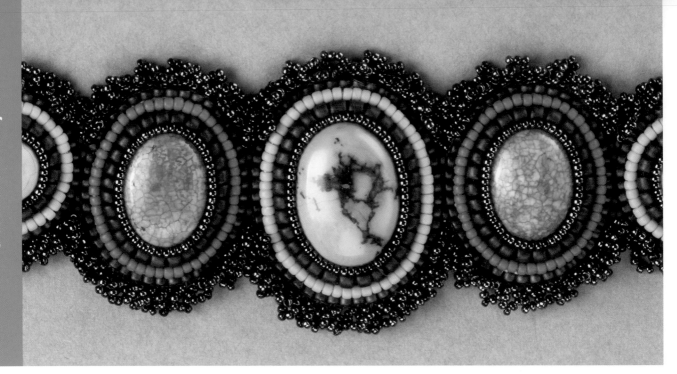

CHAPTER 7

Edge Treatment Stitches

The edge of a bead embroidery project is an integral part of the finished piece. Once you finish the surface stitching, it's time for this first stage of finishing, which is really an extension of the surface embroidery. You may mount the piece onto something else, such as a pillow, box, or purse, or let it stand on its own like a piece of jewelry.

Getting Started

1 Review the section Trim the Under-Backing (page 19), then trim the under-backing.

2 Review the section called Select and Trim the Outer-Backing and Attach It to the Under-Backing (page 19). Use those steps to apply the outer-backing.

3 Keep in mind that edge stitches are all single thread unless noted otherwise.

4 Use a comfortable length of thread—usually 2 yards (1.8 m)—and add thread as needed.

Clean Edge

Use this for a simple, finished-edge row of beads. It's perfect for situations where you don't want to enlarge the piece, but you want to protect its edge. The holes in the bead row are parallel to the edge of the piece.

WHAT YOU DO

1 Stitch from the back side to the top, leaving a 9-inch (22.9 cm) tail. Loop around the edge and stitch in the same spot again to anchor the thread.

2 Pick up one bead. Stitch from the top side to the back side, one bead length over and at least ⅛ inch (3 mm) in from the edge (figure 1a). Stitch through the loop located between the bead and the edge (figure 1b). Tighten. Repeat working your way around the edge (figures 1c and d).

3 If you're surrounding an entire piece, repeat the stitching on the first two beads that started the edge. In other words, repeat the thread path but don't add new beads. This provides the proper thread tension so the row stays straight and doesn't waver.

4 Stitch to the back side. Use a Running Stitch (page 47) to stitch over to the tail thread.

5 Use the needle and tail threads to tie a square knot (page 14). Weave in the ends and cut.

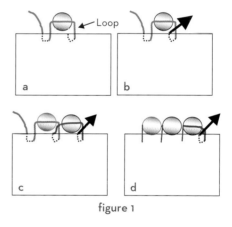

figure 1

> **tip**
>
> If there are gaps, you need to stitch the beads closer together. If the edge waves and buckles, you stitched the beads too closely.
>
> This edge doesn't lend itself to combining techniques such as adding strands or attaching to other pieces. However, you can switch easily back and forth from this stitch to the Sunshine Edge (page 65). Use the Sunshine Edge in those areas where you plan to add other beads or attachments.

Sunshine Edge

The Sunshine Edge is a row of beads that can be used as a final edge. It's also essential as the setup row for combining separate bead-embroidered pieces (page 21) and adding attachment techniques (page 79). The bead holes are sewn perpendicular to the line of the edge, and can look like rays of sunshine bursting out from the center of the beaded piece.

WHAT YOU DO

1 Add a stop bead with a 9-inch (22.9 cm) tail. Pick up one bead.

2 Stitch from the top side to the back side, at least ⅛ inch (3 mm) from the edge. Stitch up through the bead and pull (figure 2a).

3 Pick up one bead. Stitch from the top side to the back side, one bead length over and at least ⅛ inch (3 mm) in from the edge. Stitch up through the added bead and pull the thread straight out from the center of the piece to line up the bead hole (figures 2b and c).

4 Repeat step 3 for the desired length.

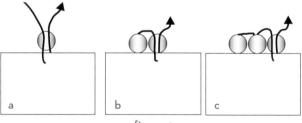

figure 2

5 If you return to the beginning, as when surrounding an entire piece, complete the edge by stitching into the first added bead. Use the tail thread (exiting the first added bead) and stitch into the last added bead. With each thread, stay on the top side after stitching into the bead, and then stitch to the back side at least ⅛ inch (3 mm) from the edge below the bead (figure 3). Use the needle and tail threads to tie a square knot (page 14). Weave in the ends and cut.

figure 3

Variations

PICOT EDGE

Start in the same way as for the Sunshine Edge (page 64). Then pick up two beads, stitch through the backing, and up through the last bead added (below).

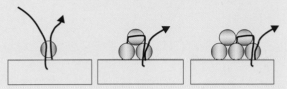

4-MM FILL

Start the same as for the Sunshine Edge (page 64), except use a 4-mm bead. Then pick up three 15° seeds and one 4-mm bead, and stitch through the backings and up through the last bead added (below).

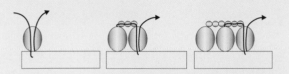

You can switch from the standard method for the Sunshine Edge row to the variations above while stitching the edge.

tip If there are gaps, the beads need to be stitched closer together. You've stitched the beads too closely together if the edge waves and buckles.

CLEAN EDGE/SUNSHINE EDGE SWITCH

You can switch from the Clean Edge to the Sunshine Edge and back. This allows you to use the Clean Edge for the main edge decoration but have the usefulness of the Sunshine Edge in strategically placed areas, such as where you want to add attachments. Bead the Clean Edge as instructed on page 63. When you're ready to switch to the Sunshine Edge row, refer to page 64. When you want to switch from the Sunshine Edge to the Clean Edge, you must first stitch a loop on the backing edge, as in step 1 on page 63, to anchor the thread. Then continue with the Clean Edge instructions.

USING THE SUNSHINE EDGE ROW

It's often the setup row for other techniques. The instructions for those other techniques reference stitching through this edge and through the backings in various ways, as illustrated.

Example 1, figures 4 and 5: Stitch through a Sunshine Edge bead staying on the back side (a). Stitch to the top side at least ⅛ inch (3 mm) from the edge (b). Stitch up through the Sunshine Edge bead (c). When completed, it looks like figure 5.

Terminology & Identification

Edge bead

Top side / Back side

Backing

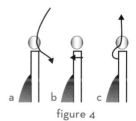

figure 4   figure 5

Example 2, figure 6: Stitch through the Sunshine Edge bead staying on the back side (a). Stitch through the backing to the top side at least ⅛ inch (3 mm) from the edge under the Sunshine Edge bead (b). Stitch from the top side to the back side under the next Sunshine Edge bead (c, d). Stitch up through that bead (e).

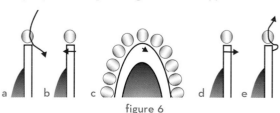

figure 6

Crown Points Edge

You can achieve a regal appearance with the Crown Points Edge. With this stitch, you surround your beaded piece with beads that taper off and resemble the points of a crown. Both 11° and 15° seed beads are used in this edge. Create the point in one color to accentuate the shape, or use a second color for the 15° beads to play up the diamond shape in the crown point.

1 Prepare the edge with the Sunshine Edge (page 64).

2 Each point is stitched on a base of three Sunshine Edge beads. Begin by stitching from the back side to the top side at least ⅛ inch (3 mm) from the edge. Stitch up through the first Sunshine Edge bead and pull the thread, leaving a 9-inch (22.9 cm) tail.

3 Pick up one 11° and one 15° seed bead. Stitch down through the second Sunshine Edge bead (figure 7).

4 Stitch up through the third Sunshine Edge bead and pick up one 11° bead. Stitch down through the middle 15° bead and the Sunshine bead below it. Then stitch up through the first Sunshine Edge bead plus the size 11° bead above it (figure 8).

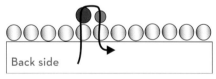

figure 7

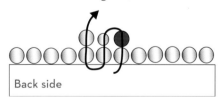

figure 8

5 Pick up three 15° beads. Stitch down through the bead above the third Sunshine Edge bead and then through the third Sunshine Edge bead. Stitch up through the first Sunshine Edge bead plus the added beads above

them (figure 9). Stitch down through the beads above the third Sunshine Edge bead and through the third Sunshine Edge bead (figure 10).

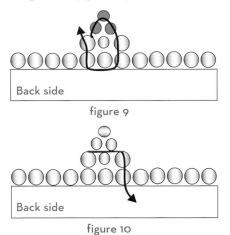

figure 9

figure 10

6 Stitch from the back side to the top side at least ⅛ inch (3 mm) from the edge, just under the third Sunshine Edge bead. Stitch from the top side to the back side at least ⅛ inch (3 mm) from the edge, just under the next Sunshine Edge bead. Stitch up through the edge bead (figure 11). Repeat steps 3 through 6 as desired.

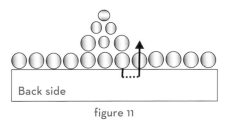

figure 11

Side Petal Edge

This edge is a beautiful finish and adds fabulous visual interest. The stitch looks like small, subtle petals and is great for adding a spark of color to the outside edge of the piece. One of its best features? It's easy and quick.

WHAT YOU DO

1 Prepare the edge with the Sunshine Edge (page 64).

2 Each section is stitched on a base of four Sunshine Edge beads. Stitch from the back side to the top side at least ⅛ inch (3 mm) from the edge. Stitch up through the first Sunshine Edge bead and pull the thread, leaving a 9-inch (22.9 cm) tail.

3 Pick up one 15° seed bead, one 11° seed bead, one 3-mm bead (round, bicone, etc.), one 11° seed bead, and one 15° seed bead.

4 Stitch down through the fourth Sunshine Edge bead (figure 12).

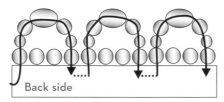

figure 12

5 Stitch from the back side to the top side at least ⅛ inch (3 mm) from the edge, just underneath the fourth Sunshine Edge bead.

6 Stitch from the top side to the back side at least ⅛ inch (3 mm) from the edge, just underneath the next Sunshine Edge bead (dotted line on figure 12). Stitch up through the Sunshine Edge bead.

7 Repeat steps 3 through 6 as needed. When you've finished, stitch through the beads again to reinforce (figure 13).

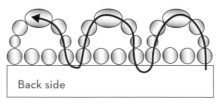

figure 13

tip You can substitute a 4-mm bead for the 3-mm bead and expand the base to five beads instead of four.

Rope Edge

This fabulous stitch extends the beadwork beyond the edge with fullness and depth. Use a monochromatic or a colorful scheme. You have the option of applying the Rope Edge around the entire piece (photo above, left), or, as in the necklace above (center), which shows sections of this stitch broken up with a Side Petal Edge (page 67).

WHAT YOU DO

1 Prepare the edge with the Sunshine Edge (page 64).

2 Use doubled thread for the loops on this edge. Stitch from the back side to the top side, at least ⅛ inch (3 mm) from the edge. Stitch up through a Sunshine Edge bead and pull the thread, leaving a 9-inch (22.9 cm) tail.

3 Pick up seven 11° seed beads.

4 Stitch down through a Sunshine Edge bead, two over from where you are.

5 Stitch up through the Sunshine Edge bead one back from where you are, staying in front of any other beads there (figures 14, 15, and 16).

6 To add stability and strength, after every four loops, use this step instead of step 5. After step 4, stitch from the back side to the top side, ⅛ inch (3 mm) from the edge, under the current Sunshine Edge bead. Stitch from the top side to the back side, at least ⅛ inch (3 mm) from the edge, under the Sunshine Edge bead one back from where you are. Then stitch up through the Sunshine Edge bead, staying in front of any beads there (figure 17).

7 Repeat steps 3 through 6 for the desired length.

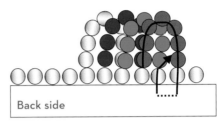

figure 17

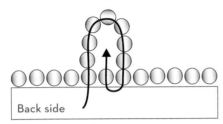

Back side

figure 14

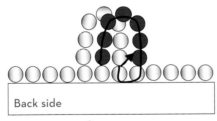

Back side

figure 15

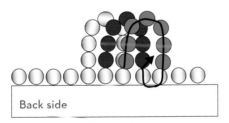

Back side

figure 16

> **tip** Replace the middle seed bead of the loop (the fourth bead) with a 3-mm bead for another fabulous look (far right photo, page 68).

Circles Edge

This stitch provides a full, almost lacy edge that adds depth and dimension. The edge is created using size 15° seed beads, and it gives a free-form personality to the piece. Use it around the entire piece or in selected areas.

WHAT YOU DO

1 Prepare the edge with the Sunshine Edge (page 64).

2 From the back side, stitch to the top side at least ⅛ inch (3 mm) from the edge, leaving a 9-inch (22.9 cm) tail. Stitch from the top side to the back side at least ⅛ inch (3 mm) from the edge under the next Sunshine Edge bead.

3 Stitch up through the Sunshine Edge bead. Pick up one 15° bead. Stitch down through the next Sunshine Edge bead, back up through the initial Sunshine Edge bead, and through the 15° bead again (figure 18).

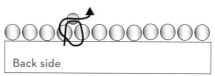

figure 18

4 Pick up seven 15° beads. Stitch through the original 15° bead added in step 3, entering though the other side of it to create a loop. Stitch down through the Sunshine Edge bead below the loop and up through the next Sunshine Edge bead (figure 19).

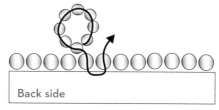

figure 19

5 Pick up one 15° bead. Stitch down through the previous Sunshine Edge bead, up through the next Sunshine Edge bead, and through the just-added 15° bead again (figure 20).

6 Pick up seven 15° beads. Stitch through the 15° bead added in step 5, entering though the other side of it to create a loop. Stitch down through the Sunshine Edge bead below (figure 21).

7 Stitch through the backing from the back side to the top side, at least ⅛ inch (3 mm) from the edge of the backings. Stitch from the top side to the back side at least ⅛ inch (3 mm) from the edge under the next Sunshine Edge bead.

8 Repeat steps 3 through 7 as needed. If desired, arrange the circles so that they're alternating one forward, one behind, around the entire edge.

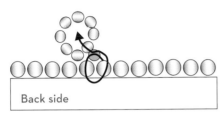

figure 20

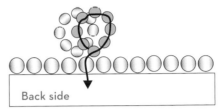

figure 21

Lace Ruffle Edge

This stitch creates the appearance of crocheted lace with a ruffled edge. The fullness of the ruffle is a function of the size of its beads compared to the size of beads used to create the Sunshine Edge row. For example, if the Sunshine Edge row was created with 11° seed beads, a ruffle stitched with 11° beads would appear more full than a ruffle beaded with 15° seed beads.

If 15° seeds were used as the Sunshine Edge row and 11° beads for the ruffle stitches, then the ruffle would be very ample indeed. The fullness of the ruffle is also based on how curved or straight the edge is. Straight lines produce a fuller ruffle than sharp curves do.

WHAT YOU DO

1 Prepare the edge with the Sunshine Edge (page 64).

2 From the back side, stitch to the top side, at least ⅛ inch (3 mm) from the edge and leaving a 9-inch (22.9 cm) tail. Stitch up through a Sunshine Edge bead.

3 Pick up three seed beads and stitch down into the next Sunshine Edge bead, staying on the back side. Stitch from the back side to the top side, at least ⅛ inch (3 mm) from the edge just beneath the Sunshine Edge bead. Then stitch from the top side to the back side, at least ⅛ inch (3 mm) from the edge just underneath the next Sunshine Edge bead (figure 22). Repeat for the entire row.

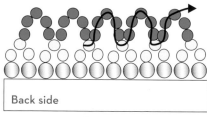

figure 22

4 Stitch up through the middle bead of the first row to start the next row.

5 Pick up five seed beads and stitch through the middle bead of the previous row (figure 23). Repeat for the entire row.

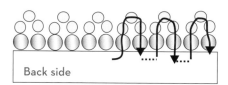

figure 23

6 Stitch up through to the middle bead of the second row, plus one more bead, to start the third row.

7 Pick up three seed beads and stitch through the middle three beads of the previous row (figure 24). Repeat for the entire row.

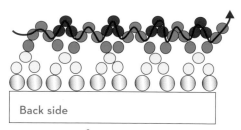

figure 24

8 Stitch up through to the middle bead of the third row to start the fourth row.

9 Pick up five seed beads and stitch through the middle bead of the previous row (figure 25). Repeat for the entire row.

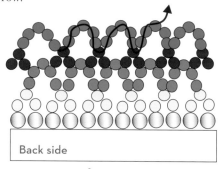

figure 25

10 Stitch up through to the middle bead of the fourth row to start the fifth row.

11 Pick up three seed beads. Stitch back through the middle bead of the fourth row to create a loop. Stitch through one more bead in the fourth row. Pick up three seed beads. Stitch through the second and third (middle) added beads in the fourth row (figure 26). Repeat for the entire row.

figure 26

12 Stitch up through to the middle bead of the fifth row to start the sixth row.

13 Pick up three seeds. Stitch through the middle of the three added beads of the fifth row (figure 27). Repeat for the entire row.

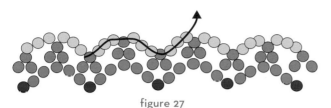

figure 27

14 Stitch through the final row again to add stability.

15 Stitch down through the beads in the ruffle to the edge bead. Stitch through the backing. Tie a knot, weave in the end, and cut. Put a needle on the tail thread and, with that thread, tie a knot, weave in the end, and cut.

Wave Edge

The Wave Edge undulates up and down for a beautiful scalloped appearance. Go with a monochromatic scheme for a lacy, flowing look, or use a multicolored scheme to provide dots of color and accentuate the wave. The Wave Edge is created with 15° seed beads. Use 11° seed beads for the wave base or substitute with 8° seed beads to increase the wave height.

WHAT YOU DO

1 Prepare the edge with the Sunshine Edge (page 64).

2 From the back side, stitch to the top side, at least ⅛ inch (3 mm) from the edge, leaving a 9-inch (22.9 cm) tail. Stitch up through a Sunshine Edge bead.

3 Pick up one 15° seed bead and stitch down through the same Sunshine Edge bead, staying on the back

side. Stitch through the backing to the top side, at least ⅛ inch (3 mm) from the edge, just under the same Sunshine Edge bead.

4 Stitch through the backings to the back side, at least ⅛ inch (3 mm) from the edge, just under the Sunshine Edge bead that's two over from where you are.

5 Pick up one 11° and one 15° seed bead. Move the beads down to the beadwork. Skip the 15° seed bead and stitch through the 11° bead and the Sunshine Edge bead below. Hold the 15° bead with one hand and pull the thread with the other to adjust the tension. Stitch through the backing to the top side, at least ⅛ inch (3 mm) from the edge and just under the same Sunshine Edge bead.

6 Stitch through the backing to the back side, at least ⅛ inch (3 mm) from the edge, just under the Sunshine Edge bead two over.

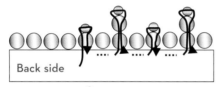

figure 28

7 Repeat steps 3 through 6 for the desired length (figure 28).

8 If returning to the beginning, use the needle and tail threads to tie a square knot (page 14). Then weave in and cut. Otherwise, knot, weave in, and cut each thread end.

9 Using doubled thread, add a stop bead with a 9-inch (22.9 cm) tail. Stitch through one of the top 15° beads added in steps 3 through 5.

10 Pick up three 15° seed beads and stitch through the next 15° bead. The 15° beads previously stitched on should lie straight out. If the bead edge bows or buckles, redo and adjust the count of beads in between from three to more or less as needed (figure 29).

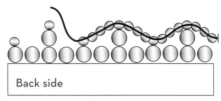

figure 29

11 Repeat step 10 for the desired length.

12 Stitch down through the edge beads to the backing. Tie a knot, weave in, and cut.

13 Remove the stop bead and put a needle on each of the tail threads. Repeat step 12 for each of the tail threads.

Free-Form Edge

The Free-Form Edge is based on the concept of "No rules, except what you and the beads want to do!" You can use a particular edge stitch around the entire edge, or mix 'em up for a more free-flowing design. Below are illustrations of various ways to attach beads to the edge. Use these for edge designs or as inspiration to create your own variation.

WHAT YOU DO

1 Each of these stitches is done as an add-on to the Sunshine Edge row (page 64), so start by beading a row of that.

2 Stitch from the back side to the top side, at least ⅛ inch (3 mm) from the edge, underneath the Sunshine Edge bead. Stitch from the top side to the back side, at least ⅛ inch (3 mm) from the edge underneath the next Sunshine Edge bead.

3 Use any one of the thread paths in figures 30 to 35. The dotted line represents a stitch under the edge bead to the top side, then over to the next edge bead and to the back side.

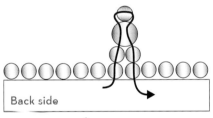

figure 30

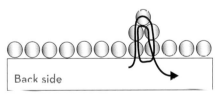

figure 31

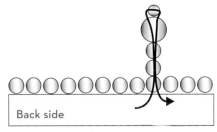

figure 32

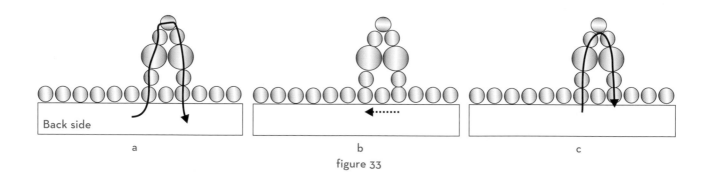

a

b

c

figure 33

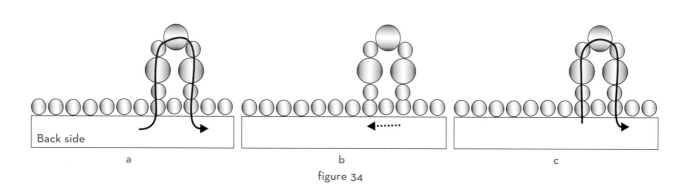

a

b

c

figure 34

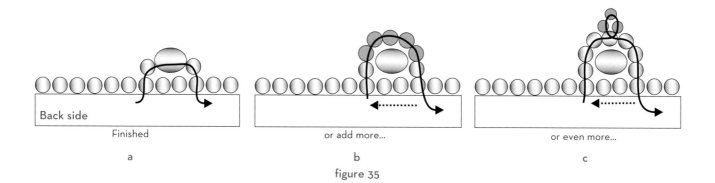

Finished

a

or add more...

b

or even more...

c

figure 35

Fringe Edge

Because fringe is so very fabulous in beadwork, a special mention is needed. Any type of fringe can be added to any bead embroidery—not just jewelry. Use sparingly for a certain dramatic effect, or go wild. As they say, "Too much fringe is almost enough!"

WHAT YOU DO

1 The best way to attach fringe is onto a Sunshine Edge row (page 64). This row provides a perfect base and allows for easy spacing of the fringes. So start by beading a row of that.

2 Use single thread for the fringe types in figures 36 and 37, and double thread for the loop fringe (figure 38).

3 To provide strength and stability, stitch into the backings after creating each fringe: stitch from the back side to the top side, at least ⅛ inch (3 mm) from the edge, underneath the current Sunshine Edge bead. Then stitch from the top side to the back side, at least ⅛ inch (3 mm) from the edge, underneath the next Sunshine Edge bead. Stitch down into the Sunshine Edge bead to set up for the next fringe.

Standard Fringe

Back side

figure 36

Branch Fringe

Back side

figure 37

Loop Fringe

Back side

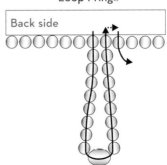

figure 38

Lazy Edge

The Lazy Stitch, discussed and illustrated in chapter 5, is also a perfect edge stitch. Use it to wrap around the edge of a piece or to appliqué a piece of beadwork onto another surface. For applying to the surface of another backing, use the same technique as the surface stitch on page 43. To use as an edge stitch, read on.

WHAT YOU DO

1 Decide the bead length you want to show. To calculate the number to pick up, double the number and add one. For example, if you want three beads to show, pick up seven (three times two, plus one). Another way to do this is to decide how wide you want the edge to be and see how many beads it takes to cover that width. Then take that number, multiply by two, and add one.

2 Using doubled thread, stitch up from the back side to the top side. Stitch in from the edge using the bead length that will show (decided in step 1).

3 Pick up the number of beads calculated in step 1. Stitch from the back side to the top side, one bead width over and in from the edge, as in step 2.

4 Repeat step 3 for the desired length (figures 39, 40, and 41).

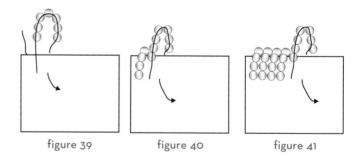

figure 39   figure 40   figure 41

CHAPTER 8

Attachment Stitches

Many designs combine beaded pieces with a necklace strand or bracelet beads to create beautiful jewelry. Picture a bead-embroidered creation hanging from a rod like an elegant tapestry decorating a home, for example. The attachment itself is a part of the design process that can complete and enhance your total design vision. The methods described in this chapter attach bead-embroidered pieces to other objects and complete your design with flair.

Herringbone Loop Bail Attachment

This attachment method creates a loop that other elements can go through. For example, you can string through a strand of beads for a necklace, or a pole to hang a bead-embroidered tapestry. The loop can be straight up, using only two sunshine row beads, or slanted, using four sunshine row beads. Create one loop or multiple loops—the design is up to you.

WHAT YOU DO

1 Prepare the edge with the Sunshine Edge (page 64).

2 Using single thread, stitch from the back side to the top side, at least ⅛ inch (3 mm) from the edge, leaving a 9-inch (22.9 cm) tail. Stitch up through a Sunshine Edge bead.

3 Pick up two seeds and stitch down into the next Sunshine Edge bead, staying on the back side.

4 Stitch from the back side to the top side, at least ⅛ inch (3 mm) from the edge just beneath the current Sunshine Edge bead. Stitch through the backings, returning to

the back side and positioning the needle at least ⅛ inch (3 mm) from the edge just underneath the first Sunshine Edge bead. Stitch up through the Sunshine Edge bead and the added bead above it (figure 1).

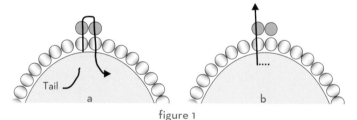

figure 1

5 Pick up two seed beads. Stitch down into the seed in the next column and up through the seed bead and added seed bead in the first column (figure 2).

6 Repeat step 5 until you have the desired length.

7 Close the loop by stitching into two Sunshine Edge beads. You can stitch into the edge beads used in the previous steps to create a straight-up loop. Or, select two other edge beads to create a slanted loop. Stitch down into the edge bead selected, staying on the back side. Stitch through the backings to the top side,

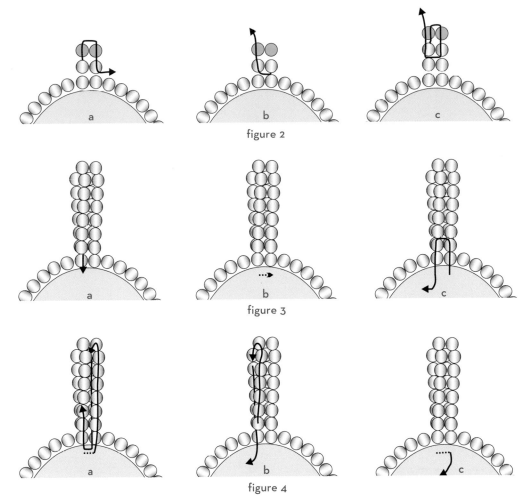

figure 2

figure 3

figure 4

positioning the needle below the Sunshine Edge bead, at least ⅛ inch (3 mm) from the edge. Stitch through the backings, returning to the back side and positioning the needle under the next Sunshine Edge bead, at least ⅛ inch (3 mm) from the edge. Stitch up through the Sunshine Edge bead and the bead just above it. Stitch down through the bead in the previous column and through the Sunshine Edge bead below it, staying on the back side (figure 3).

8 Stitch through the backing to the top side, positioning the needle just below the edge bead, at least ⅛ inch (3 mm) from the edge. Stitch through the backings, returning to the back side and positioning the needle under the other edge bead selected, at least ⅛ inch (3 mm) from the edge. Stitch up through the Sunshine Edge bead and all beads in the created loop to return to the original Sunshine Edge bead in that column. Stitch

through the Sunshine Edge bead, staying on the back side. Stitch through the backings to the top side and return to the back side under the previous Sunshine Edge bead. Stitch through the Sunshine Edge bead and all the beads in the created loop to return through the Sunshine Edge bead below, staying on the back side (figure 4). Repeat the thread path in this step again to reinforce. If desired, repeat a third time. Use the tail and needle threads to tie a square knot (page 14). Weave the ends in and cut.

Optional

Instead of stitching into the original Sunshine Edge beads, close the loop two or more beads over in the Sunshine Edge row to create a Sideways Loop.

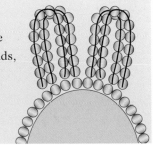

Square Stitch Bail Attachment

This stitch adds a wonderful decorative touch while also providing a practical attachment method. It can be stitched directly into the Sunshine Edge beads, as in the two examples at top left. It can also be stitched with one or more beads in between the bail and the bead-embroidered piece, as in the two examples at top right. Finally, you can use an extra-wide bail, combine additional pieces, or add fringe wherever your design senses take you!

tip This stitch works best when the bail covers a straight tube bead on the inside to hold the shape. Use any tube bead or use ⅛-inch (3 mm) copper tubing (available in the plumbing department of a hardware store) to create your own custom length.

WHAT YOU DO

1 Prepare the edge with the Sunshine Edge (page 64).

2 Select the bead, tube, or pole that will be used inside the bail.

3 Create the bail using single thread. Add a stop bead with a 9-inch (22.9 cm) tail.

4 Pick up four seeds. Stitch back through the first two to create a loop two columns wide (figure 5).

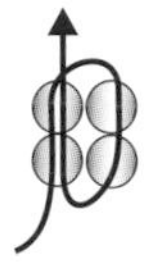

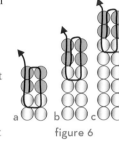

figure 5

5 Pick up four seeds. Stitch down through one seed in the next column and up through the seed in the previous column plus two of the added seeds (figure 6). Repeat until you have the length needed. Make sure the length is long enough to wrap around the insert selected in step 2.

figure 6

6 After you have the desired length, stitch down through two of the seeds in the next column. Stitch up through one bead of the previous column and up through one bead of the next column (figure 7).

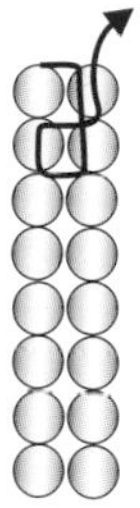

7 Pick up two seed beads. Stitch up through the one seed in the previous column that lines up with the second added seed. Stitch down through the second added seed (figure 8). Repeat until the column is complete.

figure 7

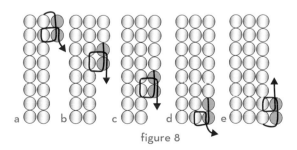

figure 8

8 Repeat step 7 to add more columns. Continue until you have the desired width. Test the width using the insert selected in step 2.

9 Attach to the beadwork using the same thread or a new thread, as desired.

10 Line up the bail with the Sunshine Edge beads.

11 Pick up beads as desired (or don't pick up any) and stitch down into the Sunshine Edge bead, staying on the back side. Stitch through the backing to the top side under the Sunshine Edge bead, at least ⅛ inch (3 mm) from the edge. Stitch up through the edge bead, the added bead(s)—if any—and through all of the bail beads, entering the other side of the bail as illustrated. Stitch down through the added bead(s) (if any) and through the Sunshine Edge bead, staying on the back side. Pull to make the bail wrap around into a loop (figure 9).

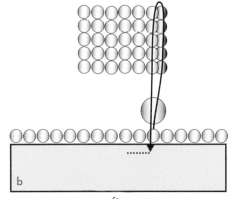

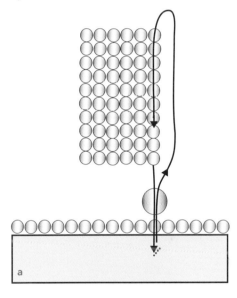

figure 9

12 Stitch through the backing to the top side just under the Sunshine Edge bead, at least ⅛ inch (3 mm) from the edge. Stitch up through the edge bead, the added bead(s) (if any), and through all beads in the bail loop. Then stitch down through the added bead(s) (if any) and through the Sunshine Edge bead, staying on the back side. Repeat if desired.

13 Stitch through the backings to the top side, just under the Sunshine Edge bead and at least ⅛ inch (3 mm) from the edge.

14 Stitch over to the next attachment spot. (If the design has no added beads, stitch over to the next column, and then stitch each column in the bail. Otherwise, space as desired.) Use the Running Stitch (page 47) at least ⅛ inch (3 mm) from the edge to travel to a space that's more than two seed beads away.

15 Repeat steps 12 through 14 until all desired attachments are done. Tie a knot. Weave the ends in and cut. Remove the stop bead and put a needle on the tail thread. Tie a knot, weave the ends in, and cut.

Don't add beads between the bail and the edge beads, or add as many beads as desired. Space the added beads evenly or in any pattern that provides the desired design effect. Typically, the added beads will line up with a bail column and a Sunshine Edge bead. However, if the design calls for the alignment between two columns and two Sunshine Edge beads, use the thread path illustrated below. The design can shift from an aligned added bead, to a centered bead, and back to an aligned bead, as shown in the illustration below.

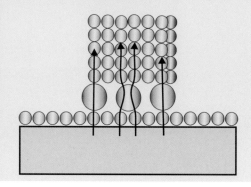

Weave the ends into the square stitched loop, weaving up and down on the front side of the bail. This will fill the holes in the beads and make them line up straight.

Added Bead Attachment

This easy-to-accomplish attachment can be designed so it looks like a continuation of the edging technique. The added bead can be lifted far from the edge, as in the first two examples at top left, or it can be stitched very close to the edge, as in the other examples. The instructions use a center bead lifted by two side beads. However, you can stitch the added bead directly to the edge with no other added beads, or even with many other added beads.

WHAT YOU DO

1 Prepare the edge with the Sunshine Edge (page 64). Select the beads to use for the bail and identify the Sunshine Edge beads to use.

2 Using single thread, stitch from the back side to the top side under one of the identified Sunshine Edge beads, at least ⅛ inch (3 mm) from the edge. Stitch up through the Sunshine Edge bead.

3 Pick up the bead(s) selected in step 1 and stitch down through the other identified Sunshine Edge beads, staying on the back side (figure 10).

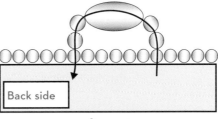

figure 10

4 Stitch through the backing to the top side under the edge bead, at least ⅛ inch (3 mm) from the edge.

5 Stitch up through the Sunshine Edge bead, the added beads, and down through the other Sunshine Edge bead, staying on the back side (figure 11).

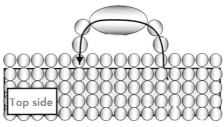

figure 11

6 Repeat steps 4 and 5 at least once more. If the piece to be held is heavy, repeat twice or more as desired.

7 Use the tail and needle threads to tie a square knot (page 14). Weave the ends in and cut. To use the bail for attaching, string through the center bead(s) (figure 12).

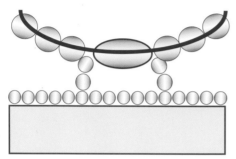

figure 12

Variations

You can do many variations of this attachment method by changing the number and sizes of beads used. Some variations are illustrated below.

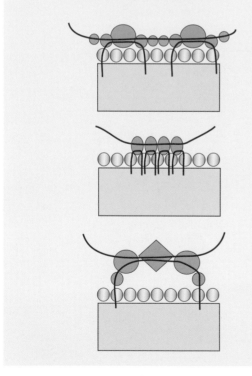

Fringed Turn Attachment

The Fringed Turn Attachment method is an easy and versatile way to finish bead-embroidered pieces. Beaded strands, like fringe, are sewn onto the edge, and the "turn bead" at the end of the fringe is used to connect with other elements, such as a bead strand. Change the bead shapes, number of beads, length of fringes, and numbers of fringes for a multitude of design alternatives.

WHAT YOU DO

1 Prepare the edge with the Sunshine Edge (page 64). Select the beads to use for the bail fringes and identify the Sunshine Edge beads to use.

2 Using single thread, stitch from the back side to the top side under one of the identified Sunshine Edge beads, at least ⅛ inch (3 mm) from the edge.

3 Stitch up through the Sunshine Edge bead.

4 Pick up the selected beads plus a turn bead. Move all the beads down to the edge. Skip the turn bead and stitch back through the added beads plus the Sunshine Edge bead below, staying on the back side. Hold the turn bead with one hand and pull the thread with the other to adjust the tension on the bail fringe.

5 Stitch through the backing to the top side, positioning the needle under the Sunshine Edge bead, at least ⅛ inch (3 mm) from the edge.

6 Repeat the thread path to reinforce. Accordingly, stitch up through the edge bead and added beads. Stitch through the turn bead and down through the added beads and the edge bead below, staying on the back side.

7 Repeat steps 5 and 6, if desired.

8 Stitch through the backing to the top side, just under the Sunshine Edge bead, at least ⅛ inch (3 mm) from the edge.

9 Stitch over to the next fringe spot. Use the Running Stitch (page 47) at least ⅛ inch (3 mm) from the edge for traveling more than two seed beads away (figure 13).

10 Repeat steps 3 through 9 until all fringes are done for the design. Tie a knot in the thread, weave the ends in, and cut. Put a needle on the tail thread. Tie a knot, weave the ends in, and cut. To use as a bail, string through the turn beads as illustrated (figure 14).

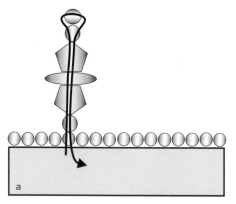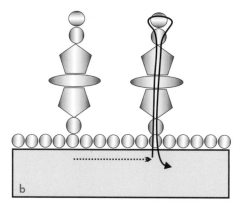

figure 13

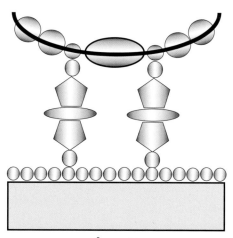

figure 14

CHAPTER 9

The Projects

These projects provide useful and beautiful ways for you to practice and refine your skills using the techniques I've already described. You can think of the previous chapters as providing a roadmap, while the projects include turn-by-turn instructions for a specific creation. So even if you don't plan to create any of the projects, they're useful to read and study since they provide a step-by-step approach to creating many particular types of jewelry.

Also be sure to look at the Photo Descriptions on page 154. This resource lists the primary stones and beads shown in the photos throughout the book, and the stitches and techniques used in each piece. It's like having hundreds of project ideas!

Classic Chic Earrings

What You Need

Beads

2 turquoise flat round/puffed coin beads or cabochons, 10 mm

4 mother-of-pearl flat oval beads, 8 x 12 mm

6 coral round beads, 4 mm

30 to 32 coral round beads, 3 mm

4 grams of 15° light gold metallic seed beads

2 grams of 15° turquoise seed beads

4 grams of 11° light gold metallic seed beads

4 grams of 11° eggshell pearl seed beads

2 pieces of under-backing, 1 x 1 inch (2.5 x 2.5 cm)

2 pieces of under-backing, 1½ x 3 inches (3.8 x 7.6 cm)

2 pieces of outer-backing, 1½ x 3 inches (3.8 x 7.6 cm)

2 gold ear wires

White or eggshell beading thread, size A or B

Glue

Scissors

Size 12 beading needle

Blank paper and pen

Pliers

Stitches Used

One-Bead Stitch, page 36

Backstitch, page 38

Picot Stitch, page 41

Clover Stitch, page 45

Plain/Standard Bezel, page 49

Sunshine Edge, page 64

Sunshine Edge with Picot Edge Variation, page 65

Side Petal Edge, page 67

Running Stitch, page 47

What You Do

1 Trace a quarter (or any coin 1 inch [2.5 cm] in diameter) on a piece of paper. Hold the paper up to the light and fold it in half, matching the traced line. Fold in half again to create quarters and determine the center. Unfold the paper and mark the fold lines. Measure 1½ inches (3.8 cm) up from the center point and 1 inch (2.5 cm) down from the center point (figure 1). Use a straightedge to draw a line from the outside edge to each

of the points just measured (figure 2). Fold in half and cut out the pattern. After cutting, trim the top and bottom points to round them out.

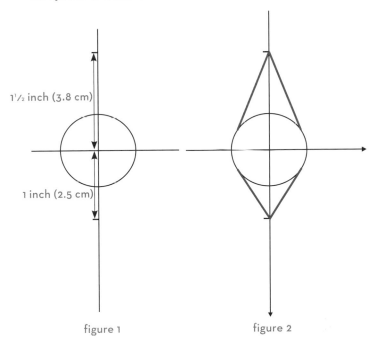

1½ inch (3.8 cm)

1 inch (2.5 cm)

figure 1   figure 2

2 Trace the pattern created above onto the 1½ x 3-inch (3.8 x 7.6 cm) under-backings. Cut the under-backings along the traced lines. Use the side with the traced line as the back of the under-backings so the trace line doesn't show through the beadwork. Place the pattern on the under-backing cutouts. Stick a pin through the center and use a pen to mark the center on the top side of each under-backing (figure 3).

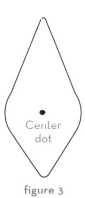

Center dot

figure 3

3 Position the 8 x 12-mm oval beads in the center of each under-backing, 4 mm apart, and glue down (figure 4). Let dry.

figure 4

4 Cut 2 yards (1.8 m) of thread and put a needle on to work single thread. Sew the beads using the One-Bead Stitch. Create a row around each of the 8 x 12-mm oval beads using the 11° light gold seed beads and the 4-6 Backstitch (figure 5). Stitch to the back side, tie a knot, weave the ends in, and cut. Repeat with the second piece. Set these pieces aside for later.

figure 5

5 Glue a 10-mm turquoise bead/cabochon to the center of each 1 x 1-inch (2.5 x 2.5 cm) under-backing. Let dry.

6 Cut 1½ yards (1.4 m) of thread and put a needle on to work single thread. If you used a bead, sew it down using the One-Bead Stitch. Create a Plain/Standard Bezel, steps 1 through 4. For the base row, use the 11° eggshell seed beads. For the bezel row, use the 15° light gold metallic seed beads. Repeat with the second piece.

7 Review the section Trim the Under-Backing on page 19 and trim the under-backings. **Optional:** Outer-backings can be added (steps 1 through 3 on page 20). These were created without an outer-backing so that no further thickness was added.

8 Take one piece. Cut 1 yard (0.9 m) of thread and put a needle on to work single thread. Create a Sunshine Edge row using the Picot Edge Variation with the 15° turquoise seed beads (figure 6).

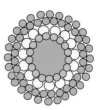

figure 6

9 Cut 2 yards (1.8 m) of thread and put a needle on to work single thread. Position the turquoise beaded piece in the center, on top of the 8 x 12-mm ovals on the earring piece (figure 7). Stitch up from the back side, through the earring backing (not through any beads), and up through the backing on the turquoise piece to the top side of the turquoise piece. Make sure you're inside the edge at least ⅛ inch (3 mm), avoiding any beads. Stitch across at least ⅛ inch (3 mm), between beads and back down through all the backings (figure 8).

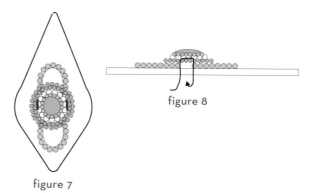

figure 8

figure 7

10 Repeat the thread path in step 9 two more times. On the back side, stitch over to the opposite side and repeat for the other side. Use the needle thread and tail thread to tie a square knot (page 14). Put a needle on the tail thread, weave in, and cut. Continue to use the needle thread.

11 Using Running Stitch, stitch directly above the top 8 x 12-mm oval bead.

12 Create a Clover Stitch using three 4-mm coral beads above the top 8 x 12-mm oval (figure 9).

13 Fill in the remaining area with the Picot Stitch, using the eggshell pearl beads.

14 Apply and trim the outer-backing using steps 1 through 3, page 20.

15 Cut 1½ yards (1.4 m) of thread and put a needle on to work single thread. Use the 11° gold metallic seed beads and stitch a Sunshine Edge row.

16 Repeat steps 8 through 15 to finish the second earring.

17 Determine the spacing for the top loop, as illustrated, and match to the other earring.

18 Cut 2 yards (1.8 m) of thread and put a needle on to work single thread. Stitch from the back side to the top side, at least ⅛ inch (3 mm) from the edge under one of the edge beads identified for the earring loop, leaving a 1-yard (0.9 m) tail. (The tail thread will be used later.) Stitch out through the edge bead. Pick up six 15° gold seed beads. Stitch down through the other Sunshine Edge bead identified for the loop, staying on the back side (figure 10). Stitch through the backings to the top side, at least ⅛ inch (3 mm) from the edge under the current Sunshine Edge bead. On the top side, stitch across to the first edge bead, stitching through the backings at least ⅛ inch (3 mm) from the edge. Repeat the stitch path that created the loop three times to reinforce. Tie a square knot with the needle thread and tail thread.

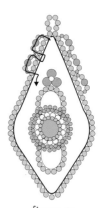

figure 9

figure 10

19 The edge is the Side Petal Edge using the 3-mm coral beads, the 15° turquoise seed beads, and the 11° gold seed beads. The base is four Sunshine Edge beads. Use the needle thread to start at one side of the top, working toward the center bottom. Put a needle on the tail thread and use it to stitch the other side (figure 11). If the center bottom is more or less than four beads, adjust the bead counts in the Side Petal Edge so that the 3-mm coral bead is positioned at the center bottom.

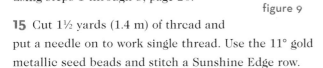

figure 11

20 Tie a square knot with the needle thread and tail threads, weave in, and cut.

21 Repeat steps 18 through 20 for the other earring.

22 For each earring, use pliers to twist open the loop on the earring finding. Insert the top loop of the earring and close.

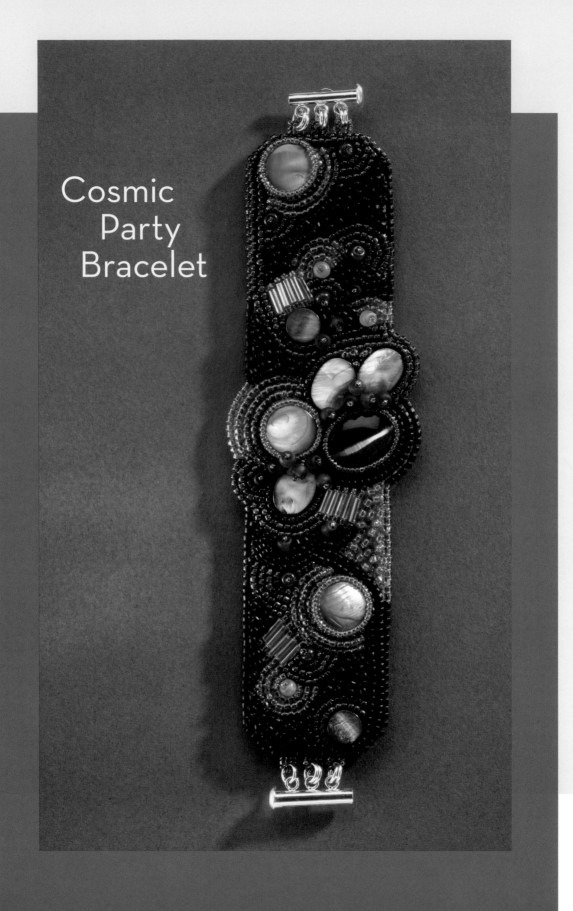

Cosmic
Party
Bracelet

What You Need

Beads

1 royal blue cat's-eye glass cabochon, 18 x 13 mm

3 green-dyed mother-of-pearl flat round beads, 12 mm

3 purple-dyed mother-of-pearl flat oval beads,
   10 x 14 mm

2 cobalt-dyed mother-of-pearl flat round beads, 8 mm

2 grams of 15° green AB seed beads

2 grams of 15° cobalt AB seed beads

10 grams of 11° matte cobalt seed beads

10 grams of 11° transparent green seed beads

10 grams of 11° purple color-lined seed beads

2 grams of 5° matte cobalt seed beads

2 grams of 5° purple seed beads

2 grams of 5° green seed beads

2 grams of transparent green AB bugle beads, 6 mm

2 pieces of 7 x 2½-inch (17.8 x 6.4 cm)
medium-weight Ultrasuede

1 piece of 7 x 2½-inch (17.8 x 6.4 cm) lightweight
iron-on interfacing

1 gold 3-hole slide clasp

12 gold jump rings, 5 mm

Blue beading thread, size A or B

Glue

Scissors

Size 12 beading needle

Pliers

Stitches Used

One-Bead Stitch, page 36

Backstitch, page 38

Picot Stitch, page 41

Loop Stitch, page 42

Lazy Stitch, page 43

Stacks Stitch, page 37

Plain/Standard Bezel, page 49

Clean Edge, page 63

Sunshine Edge, page 64

Clean Edge/Sunshine Edge Switch, page 65

Running Stitch, page 47

What You Do

1 Iron the iron-on interfacing to one of the pieces of Ultrasuede. This will provide a stable, yet flexible surface to bead on. When this style of bracelet is curved around a wrist (or a cuff form), spaces will open between the beading rows. This method of preparing the under-backing will provide a nice coloration so the spaces are not noticeable.

2 In the center of the under-backing, draw a rectangle 6 x 1¼ inches (15.2 x 3.2 cm). Mark the center.

3 Glue on the 18 x 13-mm cabochon slightly off so it rests out of the drawn rectangle as illustrated (figure 1). Let dry.

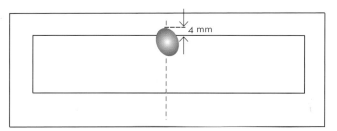

4 mm

figure 1

> **tip**
>
> In this step and subsequent steps, placement of the beads/components is not an exact science, so relax and enjoy the process. Your creation will differ slightly in bead placement, number of rows, etc. If you made this numerous times, each one would be slightly different, but your end product will look like the project example.

4 Create a Plain/Standard Bezel, steps 1 through 4, around the cabochon. For the base row, use cobalt 11° seed beads. For the bezel row, use the cobalt 15° seed beads.

5 Glue on two of the purple 10 x 14-mm ovals and one of the green 12-mm rounds as illustrated and let the glue dry. Stitch the beads on using the One-Bead Stitch (figure 2).

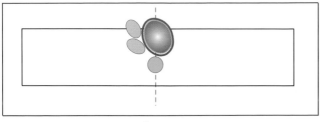

figure 2

6 Create a Plain/Standard Bezel, steps 1 through 4, around the 12-mm round. For the base row, use green 11° seed beads. For the bezel row, use the green 15° seed beads. Use the 4-6 Backstitch and stitch a row around the two ovals with the purple 11° seed beads. Use the 4-6 Backstitch and stitch another row around the blue cabochon using the cobalt 11° seed beads (figure 3).

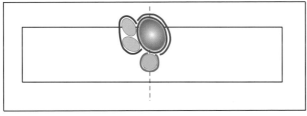

figure 3

7 Glue on the remaining purple 10 x 14-mm oval, positioning it under the cabochon as illustrated, and let dry. Stitch the bead on using the One-Bead Stitch. Then do the following, referring to figure 4:

A Use the 4-6 Backstitch and stitch a row around the oval using the purple 11° seed beads.

B Use the 4-6 Backstitch and stitch two additional rows around the green round using the green 11° seed beads.

C Use the Stacks Stitch with a purple 5° bead for the stack and a purple 11° seed for the turn bead and create one stack in the intersection of the oval and round as illustrated.

D Use the 2-3 Backstitch and create two rows around the stack using the purple 11° seed beads.

E Use the 4-6 Backstitch and create two more rows around the green round as illustrated.

F The rows should extend beyond the bracelet outline as illustrated, so add additional row(s) if needed.

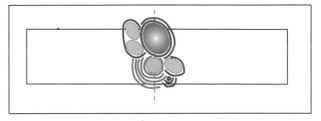

figure 4

8 The full outline of the bracelet is now determined, so trim the under-backing (page 19). Cut on the outline for areas that are blank and around the beadwork where it extends beyond the outline. Trim the corners, cutting in from the corners 5 mm, as illustrated in figure 5.

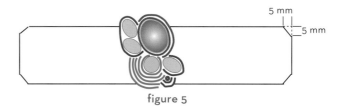

figure 5

9 Use a green 11° seed bead, one bugle, and one green 11° seed bead with the Lazy Stitch to create five stitches above the last added oval. Then, referring to figure 6, do the following:

A Use the 4-6 Backstitch and the purple 11° seed beads and create two more rows around the bottom oval.

B Use the Stacks Stitch with a cobalt 5° seed bead as the stack and a cobalt 11° seed bead as the turn bead to stitch a stack near the Lazy Stitch rows.

C Use the 2-3 Backstitch and create two rows around the stack using the cobalt 11° seed beads.

D Use the 4-6 Backstitch and create two rows from the center cluster to the right end of the bracelet (as illustrated) using the cobalt 11° seed beads.

E Use the 4-6 Backstitch and create two rows from the center cluster to the left end of the bracelet (as illustrated) using the purple 11° seed beads.

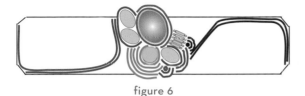

figure 6

10 Glue on the remaining two green 12-mm round beads and the two cobalt 8-mm round beads as illustrated (figure 7) and let dry. Then do the following, referring to the figure:

A Use the One-Bead Stitch and stitch on the 8-mm round on the far right.

B Use the 2-3 Backstitch and stitch two rows around it using the purple 11° seed beads.

C Stitch to the top side, into the blue Backstitch row. Insert the needle into the row and travel to the 12-mm round, and then stitch to the back side.

D Stitch the 12-mm round on using the One-Bead Stitch.

E Use the 4-6 Backstitch to create three rows around it using the green 11° seed beads.

F Create a bezel row around the 12-mm round using the 4-2 Backstitch with the green 15° seed beads. Stitch through the bezel row (around through the holes only) at least three times to strengthen the row and straighten the beads.

G Use the Picot Stitch and the green 11° seed beads and fill in the area above the blue rows toward the center cluster. Stitch over to the cobalt 8-mm round to the left of the center cluster using the Running Stitch.

H Stitch the cobalt 8-mm round on using the One-Bead Stitch.

I Use the Lazy Stitch with one green 11° seed, one bugle, and one green 11° seed and create five rows next to the cobalt 8-mm round.

J Use the Picot Stitch with the cobalt 11° seeds and fill in the area below the purple Backstitch rows toward the center cluster. Stitch to the top side, into the purple Backstitch row. Insert the needle into the row and travel to the green 12-mm round, and then stitch to the back side.

K Stitch the green 12-mm round bead on using the One-Bead Stitch.

L Use the 4-6 Backstitch and create three rows around it using the green 11° seed beads.

M Create a bezel row around the green 12-mm round using the 4-2 Backstitch with the green 15° seed beads. Stitch through the bezel row (around through the holes only) at least three times to strengthen the row and straighten the beads.

figure 7

11 Stitch over to the right of the center using the Running Stitch (or start a new thread). Use the Stacks Stitch with a cobalt 5° seed bead as the stack and a cobalt 11° seed bead as the turn bead to stitch a stack near the beginning of the blue Backstitch row. Refer to figure 8 (on page 98) as you do the following:

A Use the 2-3 Backstitch and create rows around the stack using the cobalt 11° seed beads. Add rows until you reach the bracelet edge (two or more rows).

B Use the Stacks Stitch with a purple 5° seed bead as the stack and a purple 11° seed bead as the turn bead to stitch a stack above the previous stitching.

C Use the 2-3 Backstitch and create rows around the stack using the purple 11° seed beads. Add rows until you fill the area to the green Backstitch rows.

D Use the Lazy Stitch with one green 11° seed, one bugle, and one green 11° seed and create five rows below the green 12-mm round.

figure 8

12 Use the Stacks Stitch with a purple 5° seed bead as the stack and a purple 11° seed bead as the turn bead to create a stack to the right of the Lazy Stitch rows, as illustrated. Figure 9 shows what you do next:

A Use the 2-3 Backstitch and create three rows around the stack using the purple 11° seed beads.

B Use the Stacks Stitch with a green 5° seed bead as the stack and a green 11° seed bead as the turn bead to create a stack to the right of the previous stitching.

C Use the 2-3 Backstitch and create three rows around the stack using the green 11° seed beads.

D Use the Picot Stitch with the cobalt 11° seed beads and fill in the remaining area.

figure 9

13 Stitch over to the cobalt 8-mm round to the left of the cluster using the Running Stitch. Do the following, referring to figure 10:

A Use the Stacks Stitch with a cobalt 5° seed bead as the stack and a cobalt 11° seed bead as the turn bead to create a stack above the 8-mm bead.

B Use the 2-3 Backstitch and create two rows around the stack using the cobalt 11° seed beads.

C Use the Stacks Stitch with a green 5° seed bead as the stack and a green 11° seed bead as the turn bead to create a stack above the previous stitching.

D Use the 2-3 Backstitch and create two or more rows around the stack using the green 11° seed beads. Create rows until you reach the edge of the bracelet.

E Use the Stacks Stitch with a purple 5° seed bead as the stack and a purple 11° seed bead as the turn bead to create a stack below the previous stitching.

F Use the 2-3 Backstitch and create three rows around the stack using the purple 11° seed beads.

G Use the Stacks Stitch with a cobalt 5° seed bead as the stack and a cobalt 11° seed bead as the turn bead to create a stack above the previous stitching.

H Use the 2-3 Backstitch and create two or more rows around the stack using the cobalt 11° seed beads. Create rows until you reach the edge of the bracelet.

I Use the Stacks Stitch with a green 5° seed bead as the stack and a green 11° seed bead as the turn bead to create a stack below the previous stitching.

J Use the 2-3 Backstitch and create three rows around the stack using the green 11° seed beads.

K Use the Stacks Stitch with a purple 5° seed bead as the stack and a purple 11° seed bead as the turn bead to create a stack above the previous stitching.

L Use the 2-3 Backstitch and create three rows around the stack using the purple 11° seed beads.

figure 10

14 Stitch over to the green 12-mm round to the left using the Running Stitch. Then do the following, as shown in figure 11:

A Use the Stacks Stitch with a purple 5° seed bead as the stack and a purple 11° seed bead as the turn bead to create a stack above the 12-mm round rows.

B Use the 2-3 Backstitch and create three rows around the stack using the purple 11° seed beads.

C Use the Stacks Stitch with a purple 5° seed bead as the stack and a purple 11° seed bead as the turn bead to create a stack below the green 12-mm round rows.

D Use the 2-3 Backstitch and create three rows around the stack using the purple 11° seed beads.

E Use the Picot Stitch with the cobalt 11° seed beads and fill in the remaining area.

figure 11

15 Use the Loop Stitch with the 15° cobalt seed beads to fill in the gap between the two purple 10 x 14-mm beads. Use five to seven beads in each loop, with two to four loops as needed to cover the surface (positioned as illustrated in pink in figure 12). Use the Stacks Stitch to add texture and cover the gaps between the large beads used in the center cluster. The stacks should be raised above the beaded surface, so use one to three cobalt 11° seed beads plus a cobalt 5° seed bead as the stack and a cobalt 11° seed bead as the turn bead, positioned as illustrated in dark pink in figure 12.

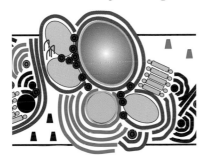

figure 12

16 Stitch to the back side, knot the thread, weave in, and cut.

17 Glue the back side of the beaded piece to the outer-backing (the other piece of Ultrasuede). Leave at least ⅛ inch (3 mm) from the edge clear of any glue. Let the glue dry, and then trim the outer-backing to match the under-backing (page 19).

18 Cut 3 yards (2.7 m) of thread and put a needle on to work single thread.

19 The edge is a combination of the Clean Edge and the Sunshine Edge (figure 13). Start on the long side with the Clean Edge. Switch to the Sunshine Edge on the ends only. Use the 11° seed beads and switch colors to match the design. Stitch around the edge to the starting point. Tie a square knot (page 14) with the needle thread and tail thread, weave in, and cut.

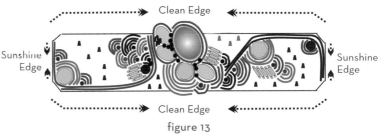

figure 13

> **tip** Make the edge beads an extension of the surface design by matching the edge bead colors with the colors on the surface design.

20 Cut 1½ yards (1.4 m) of thread and put a needle on. Move the needle to the center to work double thread.

21 Set the clasp near the edge and visually center it. Note the two beads beneath each loop to determine placement areas (figure 14, next page).

22 Stitch from the back side to the top side on one end and out through the edge bead. Pick up seven cobalt 15° seed beads and stitch down into the next edge bead, staying on the top side. Stitch through the backings to the back side at least ¼ inch (6 mm) from the edge, directly below the edge bead. Stitch out through the edge bead, through the seven added beads, and through the first edge bead, staying on the back side. Stitch through the backings to the top side at least ¼ inch (6 mm) from the edge, directly below the edge bead.

figure 14

23 Stitch over to the next loop area using the Running Stitch.

24 Repeat steps 22 and 23 for the next loop. Then repeat step 22 for the final loop. Knot the thread ends, weave in, and cut.

25 Repeat steps 20 through 24 for the other side.

26 Attach the clasp to the loops on the bracelet using two jump rings in each loop.

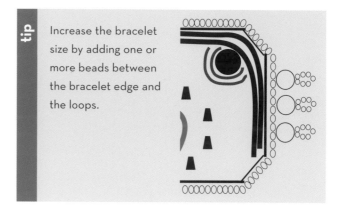

tip

Increase the bracelet size by adding one or more beads between the bracelet edge and the loops.

What You Need

Beads

8 peridot rivolis, 12 mm

6 peridot round crystals, 8 mm

24 peridot round crystals, 6 mm

73 peridot bicone crystals, 6 mm

119 peridot bicone crystals, 4 mm

98 peridot bicone crystals, 3 mm

63 gold flower rondelles, 4 mm

5 grams of 15° transparent AB light green seed beads

15 grams of 11° transparent AB light green seed beads

5 grams of 6° matte light gold seed beads

8 pieces of under-backing, 1¼ x 1¼ inches (3.2 x 3.2 cm)

8 pieces of outer-backing, 1¼ x 1¼ inches (3.2 x 3.2 cm)

1 gold hook

4 inches (10.2 cm) of gold chain with 5-mm links

4 gold jump rings, 5 mm

1 gold head pin, 2 inches (5.1 cm)

Eggshell beading thread, size A or B*

Glue

Scissors

Size 12 beading needle

Blank paper and pen

Pliers

Note: Be careful when selecting thread for transparent beads. Usually I would select green thread for a project like this, but the green thread was too dark and the line showed through the crystals. I chose not to have the thread show, so I selected eggshell. You can use green, of course; however, the design will look slightly different.

Stitches Used

Backstitch, page 38

Plain/Standard Bezel, page 49

Sunshine Edge, page 64

Free-form Edge, page 75

Loop Fringe, page 77

Running Stitch, page 47

Combining, page 21

What You Do

CREATE THE ELEMENTS

1 Create a flat back on the eight rivolis using steps 1 through 6 on page 25. Glue each to the under-backing and let dry.

2 With each rivoli, create a Plain/Standard Bezel, steps 1 through 4, using the 6° light gold seed beads for the base row. For the bezel row, use the 15° light green seed beads. Create an additional row with the 4-6 Backstitch, using the 11° light green seed beads.

3 Review the section Trim the Under-Backing on page 19. Trim the under-backing on all eight pieces.

4 Apply the outer-backing and trim for all eight pieces using steps 1 through 3 on page 20.

5 Cut 1 yard (0.9 m) of thread and put a needle on to work single thread.

6 Create a Sunshine Edge row, steps 1 through 5, using the 11° light green seed beads for each of the eight pieces. Knot the threads. Weave in and cut the tail thread, but leave the needle thread for use later.

7 Count the number of beads on the Sunshine Edge row for each piece. Generally, the count should be the same on each (from 35 to 38) because the same techniques and bead sizes were used; however, this may not be the case. Pair up the pieces so the counts are the same in each pair. If you end up with a pair(s) that is not the same count, keep track of that pair(s) separately.

CONNECT THE CENTER CLUSTER

8 Take one of the matched pairs. Use the leftover thread from one of the pieces and combine the two together as illustrated in figure 1. Use the process for combining, adding no beads with steps 3 through 6 (page 22), two beads wide. Repeat the thread path three more times to strengthen and reinforce. Stitch to the back side, knot, weave in, and cut.

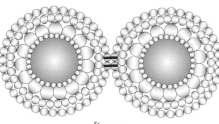

figure 1

9 If you have a mismatched pair, use it for this step. Otherwise, select another matched pair. Use the leftover thread from one of the pieces and combine each to the section created in the step above as shown in figure 2. Note that there are four beads on each section between the beads that are used to combine. Use the process for combining, adding no beads with steps 3 through 6, two beads wide. Repeat the thread path three more times to strengthen and reinforce. Stitch to the back side, knot, weave in, and cut.

figure 2

10 Weave in the remaining threads on each of the remaining rivolis and cut.

CONNECT CENTER CLUSTER TO SIDES

11 Cut 3 yards (2.7 m) of thread and put a needle on. Move the needle to the center to work double thread.

12 Take one of the matched pairs. Use one to combine with the piece created in the steps above, with beads added in between. Stitch from the back side to the top side at least ¼ inch (6 mm) from the edge under one of the edge beads.

13 Stitch out through the edge bead. Pick up one 11° seed bead, one 6-mm bicone, one 4-mm rondelle, one 6-mm round, one 4-mm rondelle, one 6-mm bicone, and one 11° seed.

14 Refer to figure 3 (next page) as you bead steps 14 through 17. Stitch through the edge bead on the previous section indicated in the illustration, staying on the back side. Start at the 11th bead up from the combination point for the first strand. For subsequent strands, skip the number of beads as illustrated in yellow. Stitch through the backings to the top side at least ¼ inch (6 mm) from the edge under the edge bead. Look at the top side to see where the needle is positioned, stitching under any beads there, and then out the Sunshine Edge bead.

15 Stitch through the added beads in the previous step to return to the edge bead in the new section. Stitch through that bead, staying on the back side. Stitch through the backings to the top side.

16 Stitch through the backings, returning to the back side, at least ¼ inch (6 mm) from the edge, and under the edge bead two over, as illustrated. Look at the top side as you do this stitch so you don't interfere with any beads there.

17 For the remaining six combination strands (in order, top to bottom) repeat steps 13 through 16, substituting the beads in step 13 with the beads below and as illustrated in figure 3:

A Pick up one 11° seed bead, one 6-mm bicone, one 4-mm rondelle, one 6-mm round, one 4-mm rondelle, one 6-mm bicone, and one 11° seed.

B Pick up one 11° seed, one 4-mm bicone, one 6-mm bicone, one 4-mm rondelle, one 6-mm round, one 4-mm rondelle, one 6-mm bicone, one 4-mm bicone, and one 11° seed.

C Pick up one 11° seed, one 3-mm bicone, one 11° seed, one 4-mm bicone, one 6-mm bicone, one 4-mm rondelle, one 6-mm round, one 4-mm rondelle, one 6-mm bicone, one 4-mm bicone, and one 11° seed.

D Pick up one 11° seed, two 3-mm bicones, one 4-mm bicone, one 11° seed, one 4-mm bicone, one 6-mm bicone, one 4-mm rondelle, one 6-mm round, one 4-mm bicone, one 6-mm bicone, one 4-mm bicone, and one 11° seed.

E Pick up one 11° seed, four 3-mm bicones, one 11° seed, three 4-mm bicones, one 6-mm bicone, one 4-mm rondelle, one 6-mm round, one 4-mm rondelle, one 6-mm bicone, two 4-mm bicones, one 11° seed, and one 3-mm bicone.

F Pick up one 11° seed, six 3-mm bicones, one 11° seed, five 4-mm bicones, one 6-mm bicone, one 4-mm rondelle, one 6-mm round, one 4-mm rondelle, one 6-mm bicone, three 4-mm bicones, one 11° seed, and two 3-mm bicones.

● 11° seed bead
◆ 3-mm bicone
◆ 4-mm bicone
◆ 6-mm bicone
— 4-mm rondelle
● 6-mm round

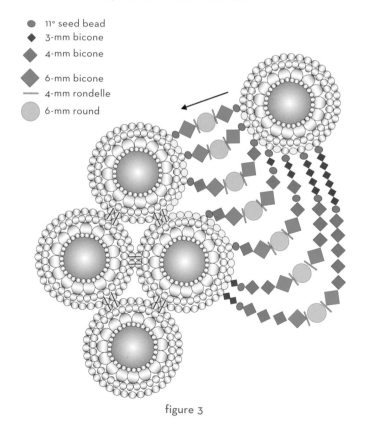

figure 3

18 Stitch through the backings to the top side. Approximately ⅛ inch (3 mm) over, stitch through the backings, returning to the back side. Cut the thread near the needle. Use one of the threads and stitch through the backings to the top side, approximately ⅛ inch (3 mm) over, and then return to the back side. Tie a square knot (page 14) with the two thread ends, weave in, and cut.

19 Put a needle on each of the tail threads. Use one of the threads and stitch through the backings to the top side, approximately ¼ inch (6 mm) over, and then return to the back side. Tie a square knot with the two thread ends, weave in, and cut.

20 Repeat steps 11 to 19, using the other rivoli in the pair on the other side.

EXTEND SIDES

21 Cut 2 yards (1.8 m) of thread and put a needle on. Move the needle to the center to work double thread.

22 Attach one of the remaining rivolis to the piece created in the steps above, with beads added in between. Stitch from the back side to the top side at least ¼ inch (6 mm) from the edge under one of the edge beads.

23 Stitch out through the edge bead. Pick up one 11° seed, one 4-mm bicone, one 11° seed, one 6-mm bicone, one 4-mm rondelle, one 6-mm round, one 4-mm rondelle, one 6-mm bicone, one 11° seed, one 4-mm bicone, and one 11° seed. Repeat steps 14 through 16, referring to figure 4 instead of figure 3.

24 Repeat step 23 for the remaining four combination strands (in order top to bottom), substituting the beads in step 23 with the beads below, as shown in figure 4:

A Pick up two 11° seeds, one 4-mm bicone, one 11°, one 6-mm bicone, one 4-mm rondelle, one 6-mm round, one 4-mm rondelle, one 6-mm bicone, one 11° seed, one 4-mm bicone, and one 11° seed.

B Pick up one 11°, one 3-mm bicone, one 11° seed, one 4-mm bicone, one 6-mm bicone, one 4-mm rondelle, one 6-mm round, one 4-mm rondelle, one

6-mm bicone, one 4-mm bicone, one 11° seed, one 3-mm bicone, and one 11° seed.

C Pick up one 11° seed, two 3-mm bicones, one 11°, two 4-mm bicones, one 6-mm bicone, one 4-mm rondelle, one 6-mm round, one 4-mm rondelle, one 6-mm bicone, two 4-mm bicones, one 11° seed, two 3-mm bicones, and one 11° seed.

D Pick up two 11° seeds, two 3-mm bicones, one 11° seed, one 4-mm bicone, one 11° seed, one 4-mm bicone, one 11° seed, one 4-mm bicone, one 6-mm bicone, one 4-mm rondelle, one 6-mm round, one 4-mm rondelle, one 6-mm bicone, one 4-mm bicone, one 11° seed, one 4-mm bicone, one 11° seed, one 4-mm bicone, one 11° seed, two 3-mm bicones, and one 11° seed.

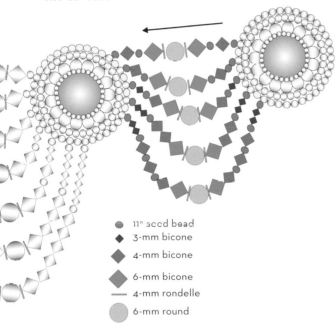

● 11° seed bead
◆ 3-mm bicone
◆ 4-mm bicone
◆ 6-mm bicone
— 4-mm rondelle
● 6-mm round

figure 4

25 Stitch through the backings to the top side. Approximately ¼ inch (6 mm) over, stitch through the backings, returning to the back side. Cut the thread near the needle. Use one of the threads and stitch through the backings to the top side, approximately ¼ inch (6 mm) over, and then return to the back side. Tie a square knot with the two thread ends, weave in, and cut.

26 Put a needle on each of the tail threads. Use one of the threads and stitch through the backings to the top side, approximately ¼ inch (6 mm) over, and then return to the back side. Tie a square knot with the two thread ends, weave in, and cut.

27 Repeat steps 21 through 26 using the other rivoli in the pair on the other side.

ADD BACK NECKLACE

28 Cut 2 yards (1.8 m) of thread and put a needle on. Move the needle to the center to work double thread. Add a stop bead with a 9-inch (22.9 cm) tail. Pick up one 6° light gold seed bead.

29 Refer to figure 5 for steps 29 to 34. Pick up one 6-mm bicone, one 4-mm rondelle, one 8-mm round, one 4-mm rondelle, and one 6-mm bicone.

30 Pick up one 11° seed and repeat step 29. Pick up one 11° seed and repeat step 29 again.

31 Pick up one 4-mm rondelle and four 11° seed beads.

32 Stitch through the edge bead indicated on the illustration, staying on the back side. The edge bead is the eleventh bead on the top, counting from the combination strand.

33 Stitch through the backings to the top side at least ¼ inch (6 mm) from the edge under the edge bead. Stitch through the backings, returning to the back side, and position the needle at least ¼ inch (6 mm) from the edge, below the edge bead and two over. Look at the top side so you don't interfere with any beads there. Stitch out through the edge bead.

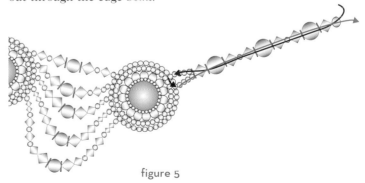

figure 5

37 As shown in figure 7, use the needle thread and tail threads to tie a square knot (page 15, steps 2 to 5). Put needles on the tail threads and weave down into the strand approximately 2 inches (5.1 cm).

38 Stitch through the added loop again and down the bead strand to one side of the Sunshine Edge beads. Stitch through the edge bead, staying on the back side.

39 Repeat step 33.

40 Stitch through the four 11° beads above and down through the other set of four 11° seed beads and through the edge bead below, staying on the back side.

41 Repeat step 25 to end the thread.

42 Repeat steps 28 through 41 for the other side of the necklace.

43 Put one 6-mm bicone, one 4-mm rondelle, and one 4-mm bicone on the head pin. Using pliers, cut and bend the wire to attach to the piece of chain.

44 Use the jump rings to attach the hook to the loop on one end and the chain to the loop on the other end.

ADD FRINGE

45 Cut 3½ yards (3.2 m) of thread and put a needle on. Move the needle to the center to work double thread. Add a stop bead with a 9-inch (22.9 cm) tail.

46 Create the Loop Fringe positioning as follows. Fringes 1, 2, 10, and 11 will be attached to the edge beads nearest the combination loop as illustrated (figure 8). Skip the remaining beads on the section. For strands 3 through 9, position in the center on the bottom section. First, determine the center by counting the beads from the attachment stitches on each side, counting toward the bottom. The center is either between two beads (an even-numbered count) or a center bead (an odd-numbered count). If the center is between two beads, position according to the diagram, except ignore the red bead.

34 Pick up four 11° seeds and stitch back through the beads added in the steps above.

35 Remove the stop bead. Pull on all the thread ends to adjust the tension.

36 Pick up thirteen 11° seed beads. Stitch through the added beads again to create a loop (figure 6).

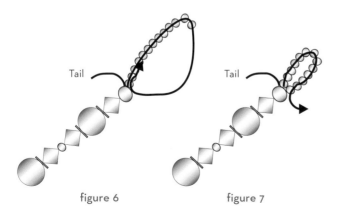

Tail

Tail

figure 6

figure 7

47 Stitch down through the edge bead and pick up beads as indicated on the Fringe Chart. Stitch up through the next edge bead, staying on the back side.

48 Stitch through the backings to the top side at least ¼ inch (6 mm) from the edge above the edge bead. Stitch through the backings, returning to the back side, positioning the needle at least ¼ inch (6 mm) from the edge above the next edge bead. Or, use the Running Stitch to travel to the next edge beads where there will be fringe.

49 Repeat steps 25 and 26 to end the threads.

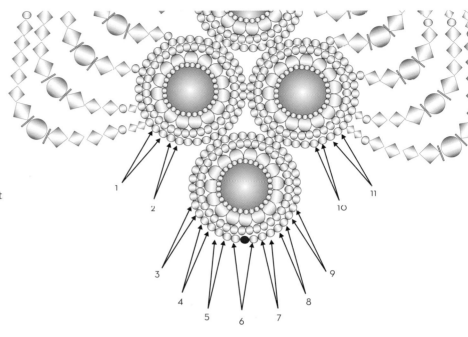

figure 8

Fringe Chart

The Loop Fringe in this project has a bottom segment of crystal beads with seed beads up the loop on each side. When using a bottom segment, think of the loop as three segments:

- The strand farthest from the center of the necklace

- The bottom segment

- The strand nearest the center of the necklace

Each of the strand sides is attached to a Sunshine Edge bead. Usually the strands (segments 1 and 3) are the same length. However, when the edge bead for one strand is elevated above the edge bead for the other strand (as is the case with fringe number 9), you need to adjust the bead counts in the strands so that the bottom segment will drape properly.

Bottom segment: two 3-mm bicones, two 4-mm bicones, one 6-mm bicone, two 4-mm bicones, two 3-mm bicones

Use 11° seed beads for the strands below:

Loop Number	Bead Count for Strand Farthest from Center	Bead Count for Strand Nearest to Center
1, 11	16	16
2, 10	13	13
3, 9	11	10
4, 8	12	11
5, 7	12	12
6	13	13

If there's a center bead as indicated by a red bead in figure 8, do a Standard Fringe (page 77) in that bead. Pick up six 11° seeds, two 3-mm bicones, two 4-mm bicones, one 6-mm bicone, and one 11° seed (turn bead) for that fringe.

Woodland Secrets Purse

What You Need

Beads

- 1 green opal puffed triangle bead, 30 x 30 mm
- 1 rhyolite flat marquis bead, 30 x 15 mm
- 1 rhyolite flat round bead, 20 mm
- 1 autumn jasper leaf bead, 12 x 16 mm
- 5 unakite tube beads, 4 x 14 mm
- 7 light bronze flower bead-cap beads, 8 x 3 mm
- 14 to 16 dark olive oval pearls, 7 x 5 mm
- 2 grams of 15° light bronze metallic seed beads
- 5 grams of 15° metallic dark olive seed beads
- 2 grams of 15° light olive luster seed beads
- 10 grams of 11° transparent olive seed beads
- 30 grams of 11° opaque olive seed beads
- 10 grams of 11° transparent matte olive seed beads
- 2 grams of 11° metallic light bronze seed beads
- 4 grams of 8° light moss with yellow lining seed beads
- Seven 5° metallic olive seed beads
- 2 grams of metallic light bronze bugle beads, 7 mm

1 piece of 16 x 8½-inch (40.6 x 21.6 cm) olive green light- or medium-weight suede leather or Ultrasuede

1 piece of 5½ x 7½-inch (14 x 19.1 cm) under-backing

1 piece of 16 x 8½-inch (40.6 x 21.6 cm) iron-on black light- or medium-weight interfacing

Transparent tape

Olive green beading thread, size A or B

Glue

Scissors

Size 12 beading needle

Blank paper and pen

Stitches Used

What You Do

1 To create the pattern for the purse base, take two pieces of 8½ x 11-inch (21.6 x 27.9 cm) paper and line them up so the area is 16 x 8½ inches (40.6 x 21.6 cm). Tape them together. On the left side, mark a point that is 13½ inches (34.3 cm) down. On the right side, mark a point that is 14 inches (35.6 cm) down. Mark 2¼ inches (5.7 cm) in from the 13½-inch (34.3 cm) side. Connect the markings as illustrated (figure 1).

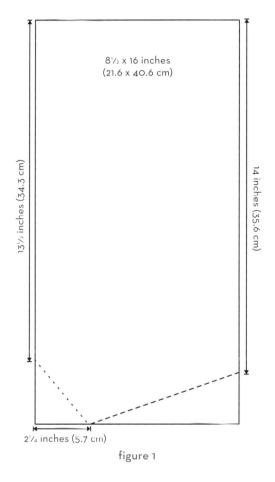

8½ x 16 inches
(21.6 x 40.6 cm)

13½ inches (34.3 cm)

14 inches (35.6 cm)

2¼ inches (5.7 cm)

figure 1

2 Cut on the lines drawn. Place on the suede, trace, and cut out. Cut carefully so the lines are straight and the ink from the tracing is cut off.

3 Take another piece of 8½ x 11-inch (21.6 x 27.9 cm) paper and trim it into a rectangle that's 8½ x 4¼ inches (21.6 x 10.8 cm).

4 Mark the paper as follows (figure 2):

½ inch (1.3 cm) in from the left on the bottom

2¼ inches (5.7 cm) in from the left on the bottom

1½ inches (3.8 cm) in from the right on the bottom

2½ inches (6.4 cm) up from the bottom on the left side

1¾ inches (4.4 cm) up from the bottom on the right side

2¾ inches (7 cm) in from the left on the top

First mark the dotted lines. Next connect the red lines, and then connect the blue lines as illustrated.

5 Cut out the center area. Place it on the 5½ x 7½-inch (14 x 19.1 cm) under-backing, trace it, and cut it out.

6 Glue the triangle bead onto the under-backing and let dry.

> **tip** In this step and subsequent ones, the placing of the beads isn't an exact science; just relax and enjoy the process. Your work will differ slightly in the number of rows, bead placement, etc. If you were to make this purse numerous times, each one would look slightly different, but your end product will capture the essence of the piece on page 108.

7 Cut 2 yards (1.8 m) of thread. Put a needle on and move the needle to the center to work double thread.

8 Stitch the triangle bead on using the One-Bead Stitch, leaving a 9-inch (22.9 cm) tail.

9 The bezel is the Outside Window Bezel, using the dark olive pearls for the base row. These are stitched on with the Couch Stitch as follows: Stitch up from the back side to the top side near the edge of the triangle.

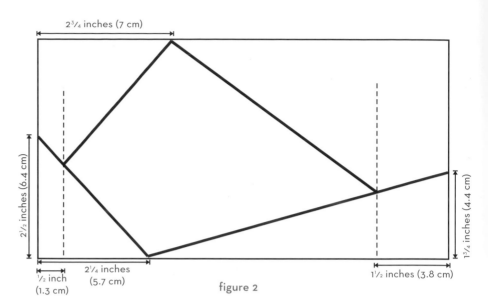

2¾ inches (7 cm)

2½ inches (6.4 cm)

½ inch (1.3 cm)

2¼ inches (5.7 cm)

1¾ inches (4.4 cm)

1½ inches (3.8 cm)

figure 2

Pick up 15 pearls. Lay the strand around the triangle to test the fit. Add or subtract a bead as needed to fit around the triangle. When fitted as desired, stitch through the beads again to create a loop, and then stitch to the back side. Tie a square knot (page 14) with the needle thread and tail threads. Weave in the ends and cut. Complete the row using the Couch Stitch.

> **tip** A fit that leaves small gaps between beads (fewer beads) is better than a fit where the strand bows out from the edge (too many beads). You can move the beads around so the gap is not obvious.

> **tip** When fitting a triangle, rectangle, or any shape with corners, try positioning a bead at each corner and fitting the other beads in between as illustrated.

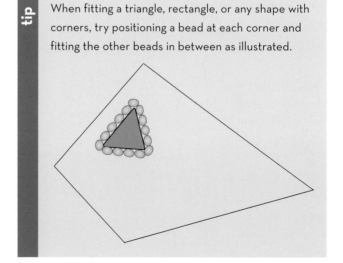

10 Cut 1½ to 2 yards (1.4 to 1.8 m) of thread (as desired) and put a needle on to work single thread. Continue to add thread as needed throughout the project.

11 Finish the Outside Window Bezel, steps 2 through 9, using nine 15° metallic dark olive beads for the stack and the 15° metallic bronze beads for the turn bead. Use the 15° metallic bronze beads for the bezel row as well (figure 3).

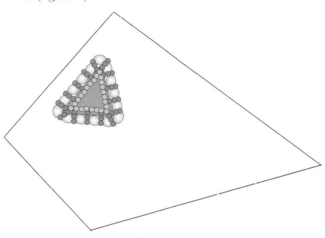

figure 3

12 Glue on the round rhyolite, leaf, and marquis beads as illustrated. Position so the bead edges are touching each other. Let dry. Sew the beads on using One-Bead Stitch (figure 4).

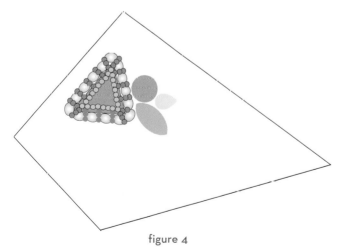

figure 4

13 Use the 8° light moss seed beads to create an outline row around all the beads using the 4-6 Backstitch.

14 Use the 15° light olive luster beads to create a bezel row around the round rhyolite, leaf, and marquis beads using the 4-2 Backstitch.

15 Draw curved lines on the backing to help you place your stitches. See the illustration for placement. Create curved areas as shown (figure 5), using the Lazy Stitch with one seed, one bugle, and one seed bead. Use the 11° light bronze metallic seed beads and bugle beads. Start the stitch at the place indicated by the arrows and use the edges to dictate the angle of the stitch.

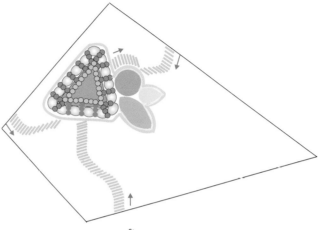

figure 5

16 Use the 11° opaque olive beads to stitch two rows around the bead cluster using the 4-6 Backstitch. Use the 11° transparent matte olive beads to create rows above the bead cluster (as illustrated) using the 4-6 Backstitch. Use the same beads and stitch and create rows along the bottom, next to the Lazy Stitch curve as illustrated (figure 6).

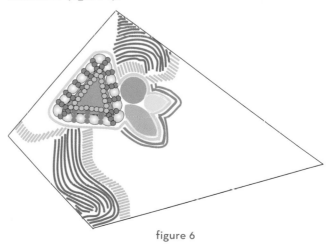

figure 6

17 Use the 11° opaque olive beads to fill in the bottom area as illustrated in figure 7, using the 4-6 Backstitch. Glue the five 4 x 14-mm unakite tube beads on the side and let dry. Sew the beads on with the One-Bead Stitch.

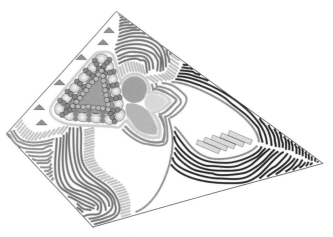

figure 9

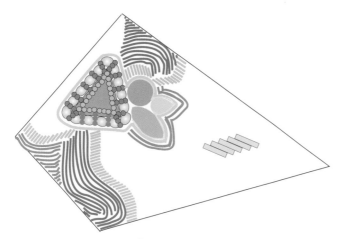

figure 7

20 Use the 11° transparent olive seed beads and the Picot Stitch to fill in the area around the five tube beads. Use the 11° opaque olive seed beads and the 4-6 Backstitch to fill in the bottom area (figure 10).

18 Use the Picot Stitch with the 11° transparent olive seed beads to fill in the area to the left as shown in figure 8. Use the 11° olive opaque seed beads and the 4-6 Backstitch to create curves to the right of the bead cluster as illustrated.

figure 10

21 Use the 11° matte olive beads and the 4-6 Backstitch to stitch three rows as illustrated (figure 11). Use the 11° transparent olive seed beads with the Picot Stitch to fill in the remaining area.

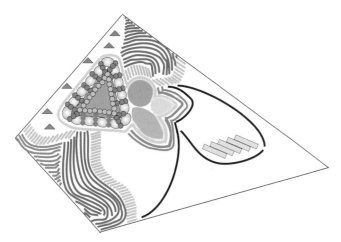

figure 8

19 Use the 4-6 Backstitch with the 11° opaque olive seed beads to fill in (figure 9).

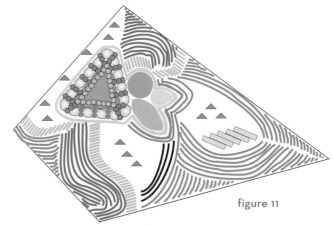

figure 11

22 Use the Stacks Stitch and stitch stacks placed as illustrated in figure 12. For each stack use one flower bead, one 5° metallic olive seed bead, and one 11° transparent matte olive bead for the turn bead. As needed, pick up one or more 11°seed beads before the stack beads to elevate the stack so that the flower sits just above the beads under it. (This is needed when the stack placement is between beads, filling gaps.)

figure 12

23 Use the 11° opaque olive beads and stitch a Sunshine Edge row on the top right and left (figure 13). Use the 11° metallic light bronze and the 15° metallic dark olive seed beads to finish the Sunshine Edge row with the Wave Edge. As you round the top corner, be sure to add more 15° beads so the row lies flat.

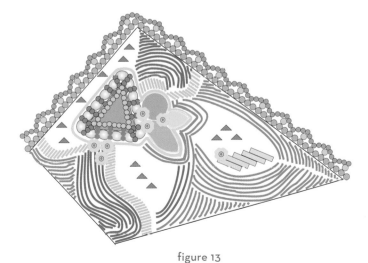

figure 13

24 Use fabric glue to glue the beaded piece to the suede piece, matching the front edge (figure 14). Let dry.

25 Cut 2 yards (1.8 m) of thread. Put a needle on and move the needle to the center to work double thread. Stitch the beaded section to the suede purse piece using the Running Stitch. Place the stitches approximately ¼ inch (6 mm) in from the edge of the beaded piece and make the stitch length approximately ½ inch (1.3 cm) long. When stitching on the top (beaded area), place the stitches in between beads. Accordingly, the stitch line will not be straight.

figure 14

26 Place the suede purse piece on the iron-on interfacing with the "waxed" area on the inside. Carefully iron the interfacing to the purse piece. Trim the interfacing to match the purse edge.

27 Fold the purse piece 5½ inches (14 cm) up from the bottom to form the purse pocket. Use a pin tip to lightly scratch the surface to reveal a line ⅛ inch (3 mm) from the edge. Use the 11° opaque olive beads to stitch the sides together with the Lazy Edge, using the scratched line as a guide. Use seven to nine seed beads for the Lazy Edge loop. Use 4 yards (3.6 m) of thread, doubled, for each side.

28 Finish the pocket front with the Clean Edge, using the 11° opaque olive beads. When you get to the side of the purse, continue with the same beads and stitch up the purse flap. Transition to the Sunshine Edge for the area covered by the beaded piece, and then transition back to the Clean Edge (figure 15). Continue stitching around the flap to return to the starting point on the purse pocket. Tie a square knot with the needle thread and tail thread. Weave in and cut.

29 Cut 2 yards (1.8 cm) of thread and put a needle on to work single thread. Complete the Wave Edge around the beaded section using the same beads as in step 23.

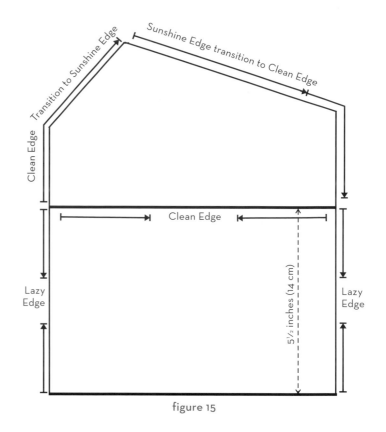

figure 15

Use the instructions above, but change the colors and placement to create your own bead-embroidered design!

Traditions in Lavender Brooch

What You Need

Beads

    1 purple quartzite, flat round bead or cabochon, 30 mm

    2 amethyst oval beads, 8 x 10 mm

    4 amethyst flat round (coin) beads, 6 mm

    18 to 22 amethyst round beads, 3 mm

    4 grams of 15° purple luster seed beads

    4 grams of 11° matte purple seed beads

    2 grams of 8° silver seed beads

1 piece of 2½ x 3½-inch (6.4 x 8.9 cm) under-backing

1 piece of 2½ x 3½-inch (6.4 x 8.9 cm) outer-backing

1 piece of 2½ x 3½-inch (6.4 x 8.9 cm) flashing

1½-inch (3.8 cm) pin back

Light purple beading thread, size A or B

Glue

Scissors

Size 12 beading needle

Blank paper and pen

Stitches Used

One-Bead Stitch, page 36

Backstitch, page 38

Twisted Bezel, page 52

Sunshine Edge, page 64

Side Petal Edge, page 67

What You Do

1 Trace the 30-mm bead/cabochon onto a piece of paper. Hold up to the light; matching the outlines, fold in half, then in half again. Open the paper and trace on the fold lines to darken them. Cut out the round shape, place it on the center of the under-backing, and trace around it. Use a straightedge and pen to trace a line onto the under-backing, extending the center fold lines of the paper as illustrated (figure 1).

2 Glue the 30-mm bead/cabochon onto the under-backing, centering it in the traced circle, and let dry.

3 Cut 2 yards (1.8 m) of thread and put a needle on to work single thread. If you used a bead versus a cabochon, sew the bead on using the One-Bead Stitch.

4 Create a Twisted Bezel. Use the 8° silver seed beads and the Backstitch for the base row (figure 2). Use two 11° purple seed beads for the stack and one 15° purple seed bead for the turn bead. Space the stacks between every three 8° beads in the base row. Count the base row beads by threes to check the spacing of the stacks. If there is one extra bead, use a spacing of four on one of the stacks. If there are two extra beads, use a spacing of four twice, one on the left side and one on the right side opposite each other (figure 3). Use the 15° beads for the bezel twist (figure 4).

5 Glue the 8 x 10-mm oval beads on each side of the circle. Use the lines drawn on the under-backing to help place in the center. Glue the 6-mm round beads on each side of the 8 x 10-mm beads. Let dry. Stitch the beads on with the One-Bead Stitch (figure 5).

6 Use the 11° seed beads and the 4-6 Backstitch to create a row around the entire design (figure 6).

7 Use the 11° seed beads and the 4-6 Backstitch to create a second row around the three added beads on each side as illustrated (figure 7).

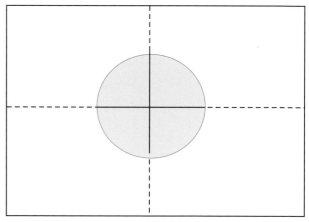

figure 1

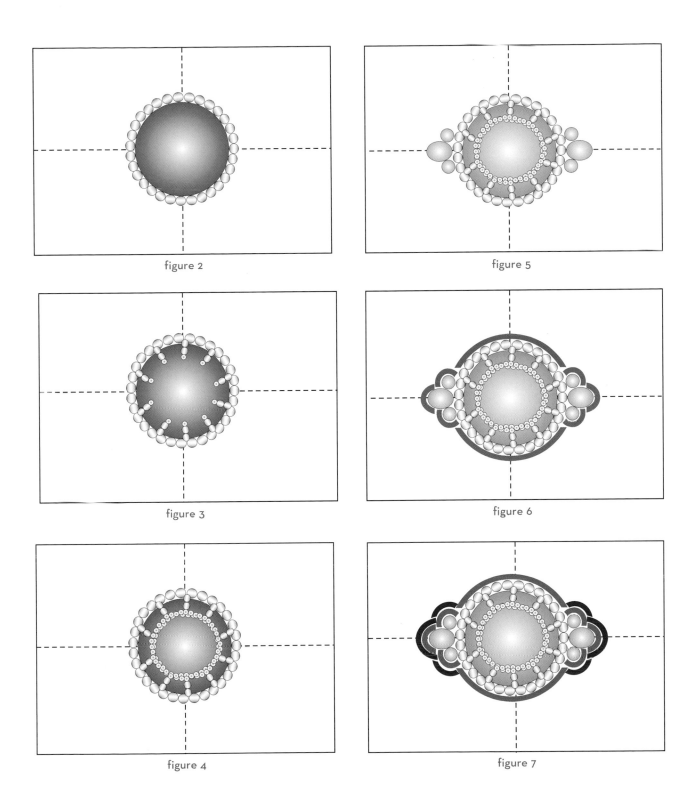

figure 2

figure 5

figure 3

figure 6

figure 4

figure 7

8 Use the 15° seed beads and the 4-2 Backstitch to create a bezel row around the 8 x 10-mm bead (figure 8).

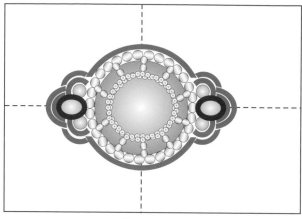

figure 8

9 Stitch to the back side. Tie a knot, weave in, and cut.

10 Review Trim the Under-Backing on page 19. Trim the under-backing around the entire beaded surface.

11 Place the trimmed beading on a piece of paper and trace around it. Draw a line at least ¼ inch (6 mm) in from the traced line and then cut on that line. This is the pattern to use for the flashing. Place the pattern on the flashing, trace, and then cut the flashing. Place the flashing against the back of the beadwork. There should be at least ¼ inch (6 mm) of edge showing around the back. Trim the flashing if necessary, and finally, glue to the under-backing, using a strong, multipurpose, flexible glue.

12 Use an epoxy glue designed for metal-to-metal gluing and glue the pin back on the flashing. Let dry.

13 Line up the outer-backing to the piece and cut holes in the outer-backing to accommodate the pin. Glue the outer-backing to the piece and let dry.

14 Trim the outer-backing to match the edge of the under-backing.

15 Cut 1½ yards (1.4 m) of thread and put a needle on to work single thread. Create a row on the edge using the Sunshine Edge, steps 1 through 5, with the 11° seed beads.

16 Cut 2 yards (1.8 m) of thread and put a needle on to work single thread. The final edge is the Side Petal Edge, steps 2 through 7 starting on page 67. This edge is created on a base of four Sunshine Edge beads. Count your Sunshine Edge beads to determine the multiples of four. If you have one extra bead, plan where to place a loop that uses a base of five. If you have two extra beads, plan to use two loops with a base of five. If you have three extra beads, plan where to put one loop with a base of three. The best place to put loops that are a different base than the standard is in a corner area or centered on the piece.

17 Stitch to the back side, knot, weave in the ends, and cut.

You don't need a closetful of purses! Just make pins in a variety of shapes and colors, and swap them out on the same basic purse to match any outfit.

Autumnal Elegance
Post Earrings

What You Need

Beads

2 green opal flat round/puffed coin beads or cabochons, 14 mm

2 dark gold shell faceted oval beads, 10 x 14 mm (or substitute with a tiger's-eye cabochon)

2 serpentine flat rectangle beads, 10 x 20 mm

2 tiger's-eye leaf beads, 8 x 10 mm

2 grams of 15° metallic dark olive seed beads

2 grams of 15° transparent root beer seed beads

2 grams of 11° transparent root beer seed beads

4 grams of 11° matte metallic dark olive seed beads

2 grams of 8° transparent root beer seed beads

1 gram of brown satin bugle beads, 7 mm

Outer-backing and under-backing pieces

6 pieces of each, 1½ x 1½ inches (3.8 x 3.8 cm)

2 pieces of each, 1 x 1 inch (2.5 x 2.5 cm)

2 post findings with 15-mm pad

2 post ear backs

Brown beading thread, size A or B

Glue

Scissors

Size 12 beading needle

Blank paper and pen

Stitches Used

One-Bead Stitch, page 36

Backstitch, page 38

Plain/Standard Bezel, page 49

Bugle Row Bezel, page 56

Bead-Across Bezel, page 58

Clean Edge, page 63

Sunshine Edge, page 64

Clean Edge/Sunshine Edge Switch, page 65

Running Stitch, page 47

What You Do

1 Glue the round, oval, and rectangular beads/cabochons to the center of the 1½ x 1½-inch (3.8 x 3.8 cm) under-backing pieces. Glue the leaf beads to the center of the 1 x 1-inch (2.5 x 2.5 cm) under-backing pieces. Let the glue dry.

2 For the round bead or cabochon, cut 2 yards (1.8 m) of thread and put a needle on to work single thread. If using a bead, sew down using the One-Bead Stitch. Create a Plain/Standard Bezel, steps 1 through 4. For the base row, use 8° root beer beads (figure 1a). For the bezel row, use the 15° olive beads (figure 1b). Knot, weave the ends in, and cut.

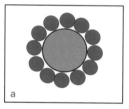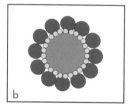

figure 1

3 For the oval bead, cut 2 yards (1.8 m) of thread and put a needle on to work single thread. If using a bead, sew down using the One-Bead Stitch. Create a Plain/Standard Bezel, steps 1 through 4. For the base row, use 8° root beer beads (figure 2a). For the bezel row, use the 15° dark olive beads (figure 2b). Create an additional row around the base row using the 11° root beer beads and the 4-6 Backstitch (figure 2c). Stitch through the row (around through the holes only) at least three times to strengthen the row and straighten the beads. Stitch to the back side, tie a knot, weave in, and cut. Put a needle on the tail thread, knot, weave in, and cut.

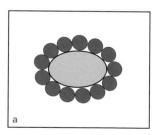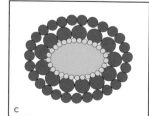

figure 2

4 For the rectangle bead, cut 2 yards (1.8 m) of thread and put a needle on to work single thread. Sew down the bead using the One-Bead Stitch. Tie a square knot (page 14) with the needle thread and tail threads. Put a needle on the tail thread, weave in, and cut.

5 The bezel row is a combination of the Bugle Row Bezel and the Bead-Across Bezel. Create the bugle row performing steps 3 through 7 of the Bugle Row Bezel using the bugle beads and the size 11° root beer seed beads. Create three rows in the center of each side (figure 3).

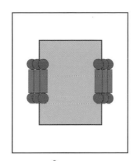

figure 3

6 Fill in a base row around the rectangle using the 11° root beer beads and the 4-2 Backstitch (figure 4). Stitch through the row, including the bugle beads (around through the holes only), two times. Stitch to the back side. As described on page 15, tie a half-hitch knot.

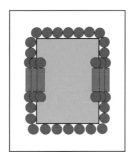

figure 4

7 Stitch over to one of the sides without a bugle row, using the Running Stitch. Create a placement for a Bead-Across Bezel, step 3, using one 11° root beer bead. Repeat for the opposite side. Stitch to the back side. Knot, weave in, and cut (figure 5).

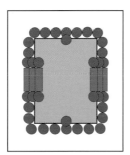

figure 5

8 Cut 1 yard (0.9 m) of thread and put a needle on to work single thread. Create the final part of the bezel using the instructions for the Bugle Row Bezel, steps 8 through 11, with the 15° root beer seed beads (figure 6).

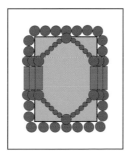

figure 6

9 For the leaf bead, cut 1½ yards (1.4 m) of thread and put a needle on to work single thread. Sew it down using the One-Bead Stitch. Create a Plain/Standard Bezel, steps 1 through 4. For the base row, use the 11° root beer beads (figure 7a). For the bezel row, use the 15° olive beads. Knot, weave in, and cut the thread ends (figure 7b).

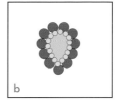

figure 7

10 Repeat steps 2 through 9 for the other earring.

11 Review Trim the Under-Backing on page 19. Trim the under-backing on all the sections.

12 Use a strong, all-purpose glue and glue a post pad to the center of each round section. *Note:* If your pad is smaller than 15 mm, create a larger pad using epoxy glue and flashing; use the process described in steps 1 through 6 on page 11.

13 Poke a hole in the center of one of the 1½ x 1½-inch (3.8 x 3.8 cm) outer-backing pieces. Place over the post and glue the outer-backing to one of the round sections. Repeat for the other round section.

14 Apply the outer-backing and trim it on the remaining sections using steps 1 through 3 on page 20, using the 1 x 1-inch (2.5 x 2.5 cm) outer-backing for the leaf sections.

15 The edge will be a combination of the Clean Edge and the Sunshine Edge using the 11° olive matte beads. Cut 1 yard (0.9 m) of thread and put a needle on to work single thread. Start with the round section. Do three Clean Edge

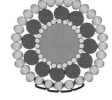

figure 8

beads, and then switch to the Sunshine Edge for five beads. Switch back to the Clean Edge, and complete the edge to the beginning (figure 8). Tie a square knot with the needle thread and tail thread. Put a needle on the tail thread, weave in, and cut. Leave the needle thread to combine the sections later.

16 Next, use the oval section. Trace the oval section onto a piece of paper. Hold the paper to the light, and fold in half, matching the outlines to determine the center. Darken the fold line with a pen and then place the beadwork on it. Use the previous beadwork section and match the middle of the Sunshine Edge beads to the middle of the component. Use a pen and gently mark on the new section where the Sunshine Edge beads start and end on the new section. Repeat these markings on the opposite side.

17 Cut 1 yard (0.9 m) of thread and put a needle on to work single thread. Start a short distance from the marked area and add the edge with the Clean Edge stitch. Switch to the Sunshine Edge for five beads between the marked areas, and then revert back to the Clean Edge to return to the start (figure 9).

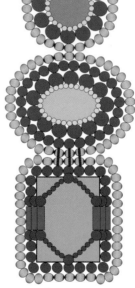

figure 9

18 Tie a square knot with the needle thread and tail threads. Put a needle on the tail thread, weave in, and cut. Leave the needle thread for use later.

19 Repeat steps 16 through 18 for the rectangle section (figure 10).

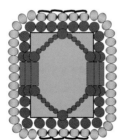

figure 10

20 Repeat steps 16 through 18 for the leaf section, except do the five-bead portion of Sunshine Edge on the top only (figure 11).

figure 11

21 Finally, combine the sections, starting with the round and oval sections. Using a leftover needle thread, stitch over to the Sunshine Edge beads using the Running Stitch. Use the process for Combining (page 22), steps 2 through 7, and attach the middle three Sunshine Edge beads. Knot, weave in, and cut (figure 12).

22 Repeat step 21 to add the rectangle section and then the leaf section (figures 13 and 14).

23 Repeat steps 15 through 22 for the other earring.

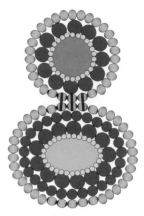

figure 12

figure 13

figure 14

Midnight Waterfall Necklace

What You Need

Beads

    1 blue and brown goldstone round bead, 25 mm

    2 goldstone oval cabochons, 12 x 16 mm

    2 black onyx round cabochons, 15 mm

    1 black onyx teardrop cabochon, 15 x 20 mm

    1 black onyx oval cabochon, 10 x 14 mm

    27 to 35 goldstone round beads, 3 mm

    7 blue and brown goldstone rondelle beads, 8 x 5 mm

    7 black onyx oval beads, 8 x 10 mm

    6-inch (15.2 cm) strand of goldstone mini chips

    3 grams of 15° metallic dark copper seed beads

    2 grams of 11° metallic dark copper seed beads

    40 grams of 11° opaque black seed beads

    3 grams of 5° opaque black seed beads

Outer-backing and under-backing

    1 piece of each, 2 x 2 inches (5.1 x 5.1 cm)

    6 pieces of each, 1½ x 1½ inches (3.8 x 3.8 cm)

1 copper hook-and-eye clasp

4 copper jump rings, 5 mm

Black beading thread, size A or B

Glue

Scissors

Size 12 beading needle

Blank paper and pen

Sticky notes

Pliers

Stitches Used

What You Do

CREATE THE COMPONENTS

1 Glue the 25-mm round bead to the center of the 2 x 2-inch (5.1 x 5.1 cm) under-backing. Glue each of the cabochons to the center of the other under-backing pieces. Let dry.

2 Cut 3 yards (2.7 m) of thread and put a needle on. Move the needle to the center to work double thread.

3 Beginning with the 25-mm piece, stitch to the backing using the One-Bead Stitch. Create a Plain/Standard Bezel, steps 1 through 4. For the base row, use the 5° opaque black seed beads. For the bezel row, use the 15° copper beads and switch to single thread. Create an additional row using the 4-6 Backstitch. For the four-bead pick up, use one 11° copper bead and three 11° black beads. Stitch through the beads (around through the holes only) at least three times to strengthen the row and straighten the beads. Stitch the thread to the back side. Knot, weave in, and cut.

4 For each of the cabochons, create a Plain/Standard Bezel, steps 1 through 4. For the base row, use 11° beads in a pattern of three black/one copper. For the bezel row, use the 15° copper beads.

5 Review Trim the Under-Backing on page 19. Trim the under-backing on all the pieces.

6 Apply the outer-backing and trim it on all the pieces using steps 1 through 3 on page 20.

7 Create a Sunshine Edge row, steps 1 through 5, using the 11° black beads for each of the pieces. Knot the threads. Weave in and cut the tail thread but leave the needle thread for later.

COMBINE THE COMPONENTS

8 Find the center top and bottom of the 25-mm round section (refer to page 15).

9 Fold a blank piece of 8½ x 11-inch (21.6 x 28 cm) paper to determine a centerline. Put the 25-mm round section in the middle, matching the beadwork center to the paper centerline. Place each of the cabochons on the paper, positioned as illustrated (figure 1). When you're satisfied with the positions, trace the outline on the paper.

10 Use the steps for Combining on page 20, stitching two or three beads wide at each junction. Join together in the order indicated on the illustration (figure 2). Repeat the thread path at least three times (a total of four) to strengthen and reinforce each junction. Use the leftover needle thread from the steps above and stitch over to the desired Sunshine Edge beads using the Running Stitch. Knot, weave in, and cut.

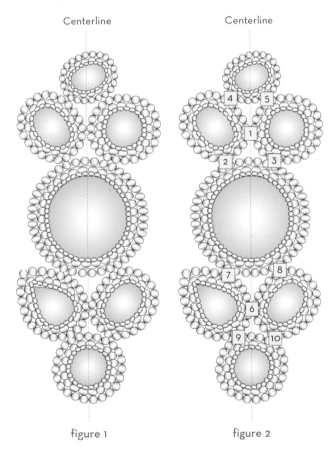

figure 1   figure 2

11 Cut 3 yards (2.7 m) of thread and put a needle on. Move the needle to the center to work double thread.

12 Add the Rope Edge, steps 2 through 7, on the 25-mm section. Substitute three size 11° black seed beads, one 3-mm goldstone bead, and three 11° black

seed beads for step 2. Start two edge beads in from junction 3 and work toward junction 8, stopping one edge bead before the junction. Knot the threads, weave in, and cut.

13 Repeat steps 11 and 12 for the other side, from junction 2 toward junction 7.

ADD THE NECKLACE SECTION ON THE LEFT

14 Cut 3 yards (2.7 m) of thread and put a needle on. Move the needle to the center to work double thread. Add a stop bead with a 9-inch (22.9 cm) tail. Pick up one 5° black seed bead.

15 Pick up one 11° black seed bead, one goldstone rondelle, one 11° black seed bead, and one black onyx oval.

16 Repeat step 15 six more times.

17 Pick up one 11° black seed bead. Identify the two edge beads on the center top and stitch into one, staying on the back side. Stitch through the backings to the top side at least ¼ inch (6 mm) in from the edge directly under the edge bead. From the top side, stitch through the backings to the back side at least ¼ inch (6 mm) from the edge directly under the other edge bead identified for the center top. Stitch out through the edge bead.

18 Pick up one 11° black seed bead. Stitch back through the beads added in steps 14 through 16 (figure 3).

19 Remove the stop bead. Pick up eleven 11° black seed beads. Pull on all the thread ends to adjust the tension. Stitch through the eleven added beads again

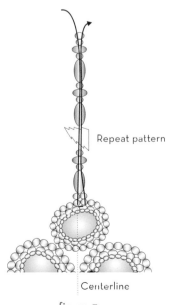

Repeat pattern

Centerline

figure 3

to create a loop. Tie a square knot (page 14) with the needle thread and tail threads. Put a needle on the tail threads and stitch down 3 to 4 inches (7.6 to 10.2 cm) into the neck strand and cut. Stitch the needle thread around the loop one more time, and then down 2 to 3 inches (5.1 to 7.6 cm) into the neck strand and cut (figures 4, 5, and 6).

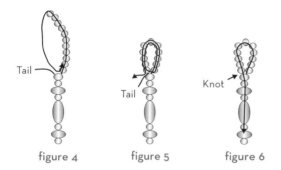

figure 4   figure 5   figure 6

ADD THE MULTISTRANDS

20 Fold a blank piece of 8½ x 11-inch (21.6 x 28 cm) paper in half to determine the center. Place the beaded piece at the top of the paper, centered on the line, and trace it. Draw a line 2½ inches (6.4 cm) from the bottom of the center round.

21 There will be 10 strands added to the bottom of the Sunshine Edge row, spaced one bead apart. Visually center and identify the beads that will have strands attached. Mark spots on the traced outline where the beads about to have strands attached are located (figure 7).

22 Cut 1½ yards (1.4 m) of thread and put a needle on. Move the needle to the center to work double thread.

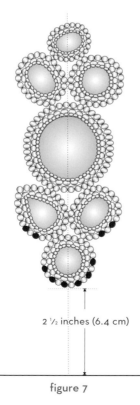

2 ½ inches (6.4 cm)

figure 7

23 Pick up four 5° black seed beads. Stitch through the first two again to create a loop. Stitch through the second two beads (figure 8).

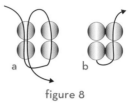

figure 8

24 Pick up two 5° black seed beads. Stitch through the previous column, then back through the current column.

25 Repeat step 24 until there are five columns (figure 9, a-c). Stitch back through the columns until the thread is near the tail thread (9d). Tie a square knot with the needle thread and tail threads. Wrap the threads in a sticky note to keep them out of the way. They'll be used later. This section is called the *end tab*.

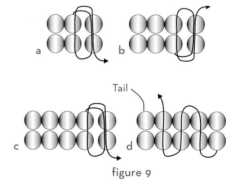

figure 9

26 The following steps will be done five times; refer to figure 10 as you work. Cut 4 yards (3.6 m) of thread and put a needle on. Move the needle to the center to work double thread. Add a stop bead with a 9-inch (22.9 cm) tail. Stitch down through the bottom bead of:

First time: the first column, then up through the second column, then down through the first column.

Second time: the second column, then up through the third column, then down through the second column.

Third time: the third column, then up through the fourth column, then down through the third column.

Forth time: the fourth column, then up through the fifth column, then down through the fourth column.

Fifth time: the fifth column, then up through the fourth column, then down through the fifth column.

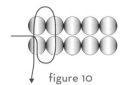

figure 10

27 Pick up enough 11° black seed beads to make a strand that measures:

First time: 10 inches (25.4 cm)
Second time: 11 inches (27.9 cm)
Third time: 12 inches (30.5 cm)
Fourth time: 13½ inches (34.3 cm)
Fifth time: 14¾ inches (37.5 cm)

28 Put a sticky note on the thread to keep that section separate. Pick up one goldstone mini chip and five 11° black seed beads. Repeat the bead pattern until you have a length equal to the distance from the 2½-inch (6.4 cm) line to the Sunshine Edge bead that will have a strand in it. Start on the right of the outline and move sequentially to the left. Push the beads together to make sure the length is accurate. Then stitch through the Sunshine Edge bead, staying on the back side. Remove the sticky note and pull. Stitch through the backings to the top side at least ¼ inch (6 mm) in from the edge directly under the bead. From the top side, stitch through the backings to the back side at least ¼ inch (6 mm) from the edge directly under the next Sunshine Edge bead to have a strand.

29 Pick up two 11° black seed beads and one goldstone mini chip. Pick up five 11° black seed beads and one goldstone mini chip, repeating this pattern (five and one) until the length is equal to the distance from the outline to the 2½-inch (6.4 cm) line. Wrap a sticky note around the thread to keep this section separate.

30 Pick up enough 11° black seed beads to make a strand that measures:

First time: 10½ inches (26.7 cm)
Second time: 11½ inches (29.2 cm)
Third time: 12½ inches (31.8 cm)
Fourth time: 14 inches (35.6 cm)
Fifth time: 15½ inches (39.4 cm)

31 Stitch up through the current column of the end tab and down through the first bead of the next column (figure 11). Remove the stop bead. Pull on both thread ends to adjust the tension.

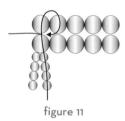

figure 11

32 Tie a square knot with the needle thread and tail thread. Weave the ends in (figure 12), approximately 1½ inches (3.8 cm) down into the strands, and cut.

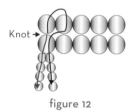

figure 12

33 Repeat steps 26 through 32 for a total of five times.

34 Unwrap the tail and needle threads from step 25. Use the needle thread and stitch down through the second column.

35 Stitch up through the first column. Pick up eleven 11° black seed beads. Stitch down through the end column and up through the previous column. Pick up three 11° black seed beads and stitch through the center three beads of the added loop. Pick up three 11° black beads and stitch down through the second column (figures 13 and 14).

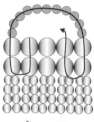 

figure 13   figure 14

36 Repeat the thread path in step 35 (don't add the beads). Repeat again to reinforce and strengthen. Tie a knot, weave in the ends, and cut.

37 Use the jump rings to attach the hook to one end and the eye to the other.

Sunset on the Beach Bracelet

What You Need

Beads

2 light carnelian agate oval cabochons, 18 x 13 mm

3 top-drilled baroque pearl flat-side beads, 15–20 mm x 18–25 mm

8 to 12 yellow jade faceted round beads, 8 mm

3 grams of 15° metallic light gold seed beads

8 grams of 15° transparent amber seed beads

10 grams of 11° transparent amber seed beads

2 grams of 11° transparent rust seed beads

1 gram of 11° metallic light gold seed beads

2 grams of 8° transparent amber seed beads

2 grams of 6° transparent amber seed beads

Outer-backing and under-backing

2 pieces of each, 1¼ x 1¼ inches (3.2 x 3.2 cm)

3 pieces of each, 2 x 2 inches (5.1 x 5.1 cm)

1 gold two-hole slide clasp

8 gold jump rings, 5 mm

Gold beading thread, size A or B

Glue

Scissors

Size 12 beading needle

Blank paper and pen

Pliers

Stitches Used

One-Bead Stitch, page 36

Backstitch, page 38

Plain/Standard Bezel, page 49

Sunshine Edge, page 64

Circles Edge, page 70

Combining, page 20

Running Stitch, page 47

What You Do

1 Glue each of the cabochons on a piece of 1¼-inch-square (3.2 x 3.2 cm) under-backing. Let dry.

2 Create a Plain/Standard Bezel, steps 1 through 4, with each of the cabochons. For the base row, use 11° beads, three amber and then one rust. Repeat the pattern around the cabochon. For the bezel row, use the 15° metallic light gold seed beads.

3 Create an additional row with the 4-6 Backstitch, using the 11° amber beads. Stitch through the row (around through the holes only) three or more times to strengthen it and straighten the beads. Stitch to the back side, knot, weave in, and cut the thread.

4 Check the back sides of the baroque pearls. If needed, create a flat back using steps 1 through 6 on page 25. Glue each of the baroque pearls onto a piece of 2 x 2-inch (5.1 x 5.1 cm) under-backing. Let dry.

5 Cut 3 yards (2.7 m) of thread and put a needle on. Move the needle to the center to work double thread.

6 Use the One-Bead Stitch to sew down one of the baroque pearls.

7 Create a Plain/Standard Bezel, steps 1 through 4, with the following exception: the edges of the pearls vary from flat to thick, so use various sizes of beads for this row. Use the 11° amber beads where the edge is flat. Use the 8° and 6° amber beads for the areas where the edge is thicker. For the bezel row, use the 15° metallic light gold and switch to single thread (figure 1).

figure 1

8 Create an additional row with the 4-6 Backstitch. Use the 11° beads, three amber and then one rust. Repeat the pattern around the piece. Stitch through the row (around through the holes only) three or more times to strengthen the row and straighten the beads. Stitch to the back side, knot, weave in, and cut the thread. Repeat steps 5 through 8 for the other two pearl beads.

9 Review Trim the Under-Backing on page 19. Trim the under-backing on all five pieces.

10 Apply the outer-backing and trim it on all five pieces using steps 1 through 3 on page 20.

11 Cut 1½ yards (1.4 cm) of thread and put a needle on to work single thread.

12 Create a Sunshine Edge row, steps 1 through 6, using the 11° amber beads for each of the five pieces. Knot the threads. Weave in and cut the tail thread, but leave the needle thread for later.

13 Line up the sections, alternating the pearls and ovals, with a pearl section in the center.

14 Visually identify the edge beads to use to combine the pieces and create the end loops as illustrated with four edge beads between the combination points and end loops (figure 2). If desired, on each section, count the beads above and below the combination points to determine that it is centered. If the count is close and visually pleasing, use those points. Adjust as needed.

15 Tie a piece of thread in each connection bead selected. This thread is used to keep track of the beads that were selected and it will be removed later.

16 Select two of the sections to be combined. Use the thread left from the Sunshine Edge stitching on one of the sections and stitch over to the combination point using a Running Stitch. Remove the temporary marking thread in that edge bead.

17 Stitch out through the edge bead. Pick up one 11° metallic light gold seed bead, one 8-mm faceted round bead, and one 11° metallic light gold seed bead. Remove the temporary marking thread on the other section.

18 Stitch through the edge bead on the opposite section, staying on the back side. Stitch through the backings to the top side, at least ¼ inch (6 mm) from the edge under the Sunshine Edge bead. Stitch out through that edge bead, stitching underneath any beads as needed to get to the edge bead. Stitch through the added 11° seed/8-mm/11° seed combination (figures 3 and 4).

19 Repeat step 18 three more times to strengthen and reinforce.

20 Stitch through the edge bead on the opposite section, staying on the back side. Stitch through the backings to the top side. Stitch through the backings again to the back side ⅛ inch (3 mm) from the current needle position.

21 Tie a half-hitch knot (page 14). Use the Running Stitch and stitch over to the next combination point. Remove the temporary marking thread in that bead.

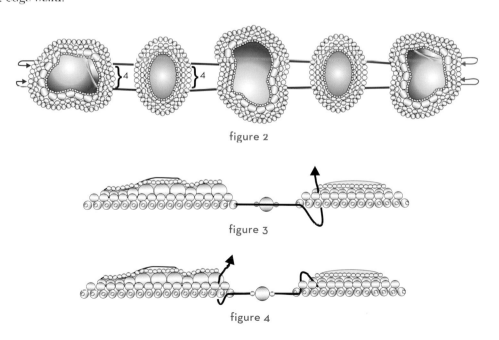

figure 2

figure 3

figure 4

Experiment with other colors
using the same instructions for
a wardrobe of beautiful bracelets.

22 Repeat steps 17 through 20 for the second combination point. Tie a knot, weave the end in, and cut.

23 Repeat steps 16 through 22 until all sections are combined.

24 Take the remaining thread end, weave in, and cut.

25 Create the Circles Edge, steps 2 through 8, starting near the top of one of the end components. Use the 15° amber beads. Create the Circles Edge around the bracelet with the exceptions noted below.

• When you reach the area where the end loops are to be placed, stitch out through the edge bead. (Need a larger size bracelet? See the tip on page 100.) Pick up seven 15° amber beads and stitch down into the next Sunshine Edge bead, staying on the back side. Stitch through the backings to the top side, at least ⅛ inch (3 mm) from the edge under the edge bead. Stitch through the backings, returning to the back side, at least ⅛ inch (3 mm) from the edge under the

previous edge bead. Repeat the thread path at least two more times to strengthen and reinforce. Use the Running Stitch to travel to the edge beads for the next loop. Repeat for the second loop, and then resume the Circles Edge stitch (figures 5, 6, and 7).

figure 5

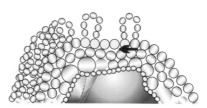

figure 6

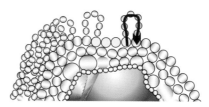

figure 7

• When you reach the edge beads combined with another section, stitch through that edge bead, plus the 11° seed/8-mm/11° seed combination. Stitch through the new section's edge bead, staying on the back side. Stitch through the backings to the top side under that edge bead, at least ⅛ inch (3 mm) in from the edge. Stitch through the backings, returning to the back side at least ⅛ inch (3 mm) from the edge under the next edge bead. Resume the Circles Edge stitch.

• Do the Circles Edge until you return to the starting point. Tie a square knot (page 14) with the needle thread and tail thread, weave in, and cut.

26 Use the jump rings to attach the clasp to the loops.

Ceremonial
Dance
Necklace

What You Need

Beads

- 1 amazonite donut, 35 mm
- 4 aqua terra jasper flat oval beads, 22 x 30 mm
- 3 aqua terra jasper flat round beads, 12 mm
- 3 tiger jasper flat oval beads, 20 x 30 mm
- 2 tiger jasper flat oval beads, 12 x 18 mm
- 1 metallic gold shank-style button, 22 mm
- 57 to 62 amazonite round beads, 6 mm
- 15 amazonite flat round beads, 8 mm
- 57 to 62 tiger jasper heishi beads, 3 x 5 mm
- 18 picture jasper rondelle beads, 4 x 6 mm
- 57 to 62 picture jasper flat round beads, 8 mm
- 1 carved bone flat-leaf bead, 15 x 33 mm
- 87 to 100 shell tan coin drops, 10 mm
- 20 turquoise chips, medium
- 10 grams of 15° metallic gold seed beads
- 20 grams of 11° matte turquoise seed beads
- 90 grams of 11° opaque tan seed beads
- 1 gram of 11° metallic gold seed beads
- 10 grams of 8° metallic gold seed beads
- 10 grams of 6° matte light gold seed beads

Outer-backing and under-backing

- 1 piece of each, 3½ x 4½ inches (8.9 x 11.4 cm)
- 7 pieces of each, 2½ x 2½ inches (6.4 x 6.4 cm)
- 2 pieces of each, 1½ x 1¾ inches (3.8 x 4.4 cm)

1 gold hook-and-eye clasp

4 gold jump rings, 5 mm

Tan beading thread, size A or B

Glue

Scissors

Size 12 beading needle

Blank paper and pen

Pliers

Sticky notes

Stitches Used

What You Do

CREATE THE CENTER SECTION

1 Fold a piece of blank paper. Referring to figure 1, draw a line near the top of the page. Mark a spot on the line that's ⅞ inch (2.2 cm) in from the fold. Mark a spot near the fold ⅛ inch (3 mm) below the line. Draw another line 3½ inches (8.9 cm) lower than the original line and mark a point on it that's 1½ inches (3.8 cm) from the fold. Mark a spot near the fold that's 3¾ inches (9.5 cm) below the original line. Now refer to figure 2. Draw a line from the top spot to the mark 1½ inches (3.8 cm) in. Draw a line from this spot to the mark on the fold. Draw a line from the top spot to the ⅛-inch (3 mm) spot on the fold.

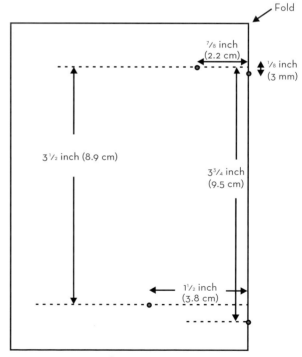

figure 1

Fold ↓

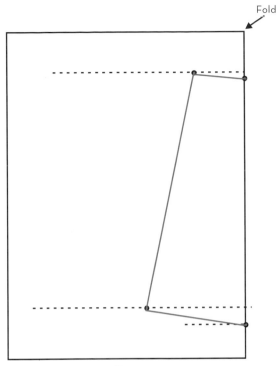

figure 2

2 Cut on the lines as illustrated. With the paper still folded, round the corners slightly.

3 Open the form and trace on the 3½ x 4½-inch (8.9 x 11.4 cm) under-backing. Cut along the traced line.

4 Glue on one 20 x 30-mm tiger jasper oval bead, one 12-mm aqua terra, and the leaf bone bead, and let dry (figure 3).

figure 3

5 Cut 2 yards (1.8 m) of thread and put a needle on. Use the One-Bead Stitch to sew the beads on.

6 Treat the group like one cabochon, and create a Plain/Standard Bezel, steps 1 through 4. Use the gold 6° seed beads for the base row. Use the gold 15° beads for the bezel row, and complete the bezel row only on the tiger jasper and aqua terra portions. Create an additional row around the base row with the Backstitch using the turquoise 11° beads.

7 Fill in the remaining area with the Backstitch using the tan 11° beads (figure 4).

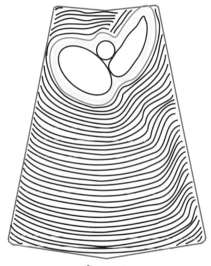

figure 4

8 Embellish the top portion with the Stacks Stitch, referring to figure 5 as you do so.

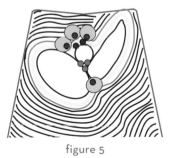

figure 5

A Use one shell coin, one turquoise chip, and a metallic gold 11° bead as the turn bead in each of the four places designated by a gold circle with a pink dot on the illustration.

B Use one turquoise chip and a metallic gold 11° bead as the turn bead in each of the two places designated with a purple dot on the illustration.

C Use gold 15° seed beads, one picture jasper rondelle, and a metallic gold 11° bead as the turn bead in each of the three places designated with a green dot on the illustration. This stack is positioned in the gap between the large focal beads. Select a quantity of 15° beads in the stack to position the top of the stack above the focal beads. Each stack may have a different count of 15° beads.

9 Glue the donut on a 2½ x 2½-inch (6.4 x 6.4 cm) backing and let dry.

10 Cut 2 yards (1.8 m) of thread and put a needle on. Move the needle to the center to work double thread.

11 Using the button and the gold 6° beads, determine the beads to use to center the button in the donut hole, and fill the hole from side to side. Stitch up from one side of the donut hole and leave a 9-inch (22.9 cm) tail. Pick up the selected beads and button. Stitch down through the backing on the other side of the donut hole. Leave a large loop. Stitch up through the backing at the original spot, through the added beads, and down through the backing on the other side of the donut hole. Now pull the needle thread and tail thread to reduce the loop and fit the beads and button into the donut hole. Tie a square knot (page 14) with the needle thread and tail threads. Weave the ends in and cut (figure 6).

12 Create a Plain/Standard Bezel, steps 1 through 4. Use the gold 6° beads for the base row and the gold 15° beads for the bezel row. Stitch an additional row with the 4-6 Backstitch using the turquoise 11° beads. Stitch through the beads (through the holes only) three or more times to strengthen the row and straighten the beads.

13 Trim the backing as discussed in Trim the Under-Backing, page 19.

14 Apply and trim the outer-backing following steps 1 through 3 on page 20.

15 Create a Sunshine Edge using the tan 11° beads.

16 Turn the piece to a desired orientation and identify a bottom middle bead. Cut 3½ yards (3.2 m) of thread and put a needle on. Stitch up through the backings above the center-bottom bead to the top side at least ⅛ inch (3 mm) from the edge. Stitch through the edge bead. Leave a tail of 1¾ yards (1.6 m, half the thread). Wrap the tail in a sticky note to keep it out of the way. Create Fringe Edge according to the Fringe Chart, starting in the center and working to the right. Knot the thread, weave in, and cut. Unwrap the tail thread and put a needle on. Finish the Fringe Edge to the left using the Fringe Chart (remember, the center is already done). Knot the thread, weave in, and cut.

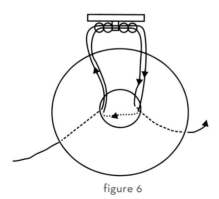

figure 6

FRINGE CHART

Fringe Column	Number of Tan 11° Beads (then add end sequence)
Center	24
7 ,9	21
6, 10	18
5, 11	15
4, 12	12
3, 13	9
2, 14	6
1, 15	3

END SEQUENCE

11° metallic gold
Picture jasper rondelle
11° metallic gold
6-mm amazonite flat round
11° metallic gold (turn bead)

17 Cut 2 yards (1.8 m) of thread and put a needle on. Create a Side Petal Edge, steps 2 through 7, using the 15°, 11°, and 8° metallic gold beads. Substitute the 8° bead for the 3-mm bead used in the steps. The edge is a four-bead base, so plan the start and finish position by counting the Sunshine Edge beads on the piece and centering the stitch, leaving beads blank as needed.

18 Cut 2 yards (1.8 m) of thread and put a needle on. Move the needle to the center to work double thread. Position the donut piece on the center section as illustrated (figure 7) and hold in place. Stitch up from the back side through all backings to the top side of the donut section, leaving a 9-inch (22.9 cm) tail. Use the Running Stitch with a stitch length of approximately ½ inch (1.3 m). Stitch up and down through both sections, around the donut piece, positioning the stitches between the base row and the turquoise additional row on the donut piece as designated by the red line on the illustration. Tie knots and weave in the threads.

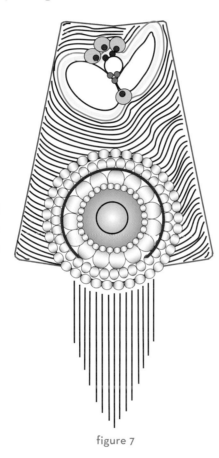

figure 7

19 Repeat steps 14 and 15 for this section. Use only the original edge of the under-backing for applying the backing and Sunshine Edge. Do not put backing or edge stitch on the donut section. Edge stitch the backing section under the donut.

20 Identify a bottom center bead on the edge underneath the donut section. Cut 7½ yards (6.8 m) of thread and put a needle on. Stitch up through the backings above the center-bottom bead to the top side at least ⅛ inch (3 mm) from the edge. Stitch out through the edge bead. Leave a tail of 3¾ yards (3.4 m, half the thread). Wrap the tail in a sticky note to keep it out of the way. Create fringe, step 3 on page 77. For the center fringe, use 55 tan 11° seed beads plus the end sequence (below). Work from the center to the right.

END SEQUENCE

▬	Tiger jasper heishi
○	11° tan
◯	6 mm amazonite round
◉	11° metallic gold
⬤	8-mm picture jasper flat round
◉	11° metallic gold (turn bead)

21 For each subsequent fringe, reduce the count of tan seed beads by two (e.g., 53, 51, 49, etc.) and add the end sequence. Repeat for all fringes to the right. Stop when you reach the corner (approximately 20 fringes from center to right). Tie a knot, weave in, and cut.

22 Unwrap the tail thread and put a needle on. Repeat step 21, except work from the center to the left.

23 Cut 2 yards (1.8 m) of thread and put a needle on.

24 Identify the top Sunshine Edge bead on each side that sits straight out. (In other words, the bead is straight with the side, not curving around the corner.) Start there and create a Herringbone Loop Bail Attachment, steps 2 through 8, using the tan 11° beads.

Make the loop 13 beads long. Create as a Sideways Loop (see the option on page 81). Leave four edge beads blank on the loop (figure 8).

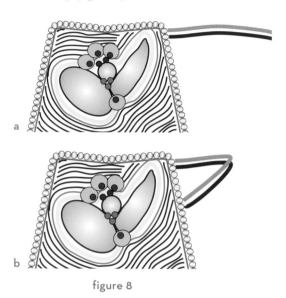

figure 8

25 Repeat step 24 just below the current loop, except make the loop 16 beads long (figure 9). Repeat on the other side, starting with step 23.

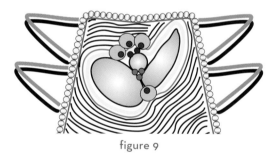

figure 9

26 Set this section aside for later.

CREATE THE REMAINING SECTIONS

27 Glue two 22 x 30-mm aqua terra beads each to a 2½ x 2½-inch (6.4 x 6.4 cm) under-backing. Let dry.

28 Using one of the sections created above, sew on using the One-Bead Stitch.

29 Repeat step 12. Then stitch two more additional rows with the Backstitch using the tan 11° beads.

30 Embellish with the Stacks Stitch, using one shell coin, one turquoise chip, and a metallic gold 11° bead as the turn bead in each of the three places designated by a gold circle with a pink dot in figure 10. Use one turquoise chip and a metallic gold 11° bead as the turn bead in each of the four places designated with a purple dot on the illustration.

figure 10

31 Repeat steps 13 through 15.

32 Find and mark the center following steps 1 through 5, page 15.

33 At the center top, count down eight beads in a clockwise direction. Start there and create a Herringbone Loop Bail Attachment, steps 2 through 8, using the tan 11° beads. Make the loop 13 beads long. Create as a Sideways Loop (see the option on page 81). Leave four edge beads blank from the top of the loop to the bottom of the loop as previously done in step 24.

34 Repeat steps 28 through 33 for the other 22 x 30-mm aqua terra bead section, except count counterclockwise on step 33.

35 Glue two 20 x 30-mm tiger jasper and two 12-mm aqua terra beads to the 2½ x 2-inch (6.4 cm) under-backing as shown (figure 11). Let dry.

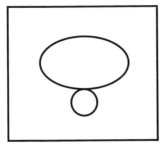

figure 11

36 Using one of the sections created above, sew both beads on using the One-Bead Stitch.

37 Repeat step 12 with the following exception. Use the gold 8° beads for the base row around the 12-mm aqua terra bead and switch back to the gold 6° beads around the tiger jasper. Then stitch one more additional row with the Backstitch using the tan 11° beads.

38 Repeat steps 13 through 15, then step 32.

39 Repeat step 33 except count nine beads clockwise from the center top.

40 Repeat steps 36 through 39 for the other section except count counterclockwise on step 39.

41 Take two 22 x 30-mm aqua terra beads and glue each to a 2½ x 2½-inch (6.4 x 6.4 cm) under-backing. Let dry.

42 Using one of the sections created above, sew on using the One-Bead Stitch.

43 Repeat step 12. Then stitch one more additional row with the Backstitch, using the tan 11° beads.

44 Repeat steps 13 through 15, then step 32.

45 Repeat step 33, except count nine beads clockwise from the center top.

46 Repeat steps 42 through 45 for the other 22 x 30-mm aqua terra bead section, except count counterclockwise on step 45.

47 Take the two 12 x 18-mm tiger jasper beads and glue each to a 1½ x 1¾-inch (3.8 x 4.4 cm) under-backing. Let dry.

48 Repeat step 12 except use the gold 8° beads for the base row. Stitch one more additional row with the Backstitch, using the tan 11° beads.

49 Repeat steps 13 through 15, then step 32.

50 Repeat step 33, except count seven beads clockwise from the center top.

51 Repeat steps 48 through 50 for the other 12 x 18-mm tiger jasper section, except count counterclockwise on step 50.

CONNECT THE SECTIONS AND ADD FRINGE

52 Take the two 22 x 30-mm aqua terra jasper sections with the stacks embellishment. Use the one with the Herringbone Loop on the right.

53 At the center top, count down six beads in a counterclockwise direction. Start there and create a Herringbone Loop Bail Attachment, steps 2 through 8, using the tan 11° beads. Make the loop 13 beads long. Create as a Sideways Loop (see the option on page 81). Leave four beads blank from the top of the loop to the bottom of the loop, as previously done in step 24. And, before attaching, string the loop through the top loop on the center section.

54 Repeat step 53, except start in the bead below the loop created in step 53 and make the loop 16 beads long (figure 12).

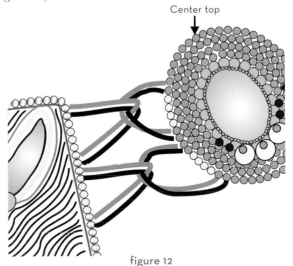

Center top

figure 12

55 Repeat steps 53 and 54 using the other aqua terra jasper section and counting clockwise.

56 Cut 3½ yards (3.2 m) of thread and put a needle on.

57 Stitch from the back side to the top side, at least ⅛ inch (3 mm) from the edge, under the third bead just below the double Herringbone Loops. Stitch out through the bead. Create Standard Fringe, step 3 on page 77. Pick up 41 tan 11° beads plus the end sequence used in step 20. For subsequent fringes, reduce the count of 11° beads by three (e.g., 41, 38, 35, 32, 29, etc.) until you have 11 fringes.

58 The remaining fringe will be Loop Fringe that requires double thread. So, stitch to the top side, but hold the thread end so it stays on the back side. Move the needle to position for double thread with a 9-inch (22.9 cm) tail. Stitch, returning to the back side. Stitch out through the next empty Sunshine Edge bead.

59 Pick up 11° beads as follows: ten tan, three turquoise, and one gold. Pick up one shell coin bead. Pick up 11° beads: one gold, three turquoise, and eleven tan. Stitch up through the next empty Sunshine Edge bead, staying on the back side. Stitch to the top side, at least ⅛ inch (3 mm) from the edge. Stitch to the back side under the next empty Sunshine Edge bead, at least ⅛ inch (3 mm) from the edge (figure 13). *Note:* The count on one side of the loop is different from the other side by one bead to compensate for the curve of the edge. This is done so that the drop hangs in the center.

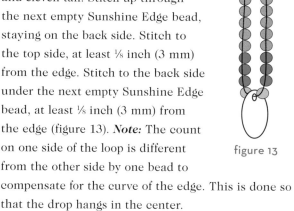

figure 13

60 Repeat step 59 for the remaining loops until you reach the Herringbone Loop on the other side. For each subsequent fringe, reduce the count of the tan seed beads by one. So, for the next loop, you should use 9-3-1-coin-1-3-10. Tie knots in the thread ends, weave in, and cut.

61 Repeat steps 56 through 60 for the other side in mirror image.

62 Take the two tiger jasper oval and aqua terra round combination sections. Use the one with the Herringbone Loop on the right. Repeat step 53, except count down nine beads in a counterclockwise direction and loop through the previously attached aqua terra section.

63 Cut 2 yards (1.8 m) of thread and put a needle on. Move the needle to the center to work double thread.

64 Stitch from the back side to the top side under the Sunshine Edge bead, at least ⅛ inch (3 mm) from the edge on the bottom circle as illustrated. Stitch out through the edge bead.

65 Pick up 11° beads as follows: three tan, two turquoise, one gold. Pick up one shell coin bead. Pick up 11° beads: one gold, two turquoise, and three tan. Stitch up through the next empty Sunshine Edge bead, staying on the back side. Stitch to the top side, at least ⅛ inch (3 mm) from the edge. Stitch, returning to the back side, at least ⅛ inch (3 mm) from the edge under the next empty Sunshine Edge bead. Repeat on the bottom curved section. Tie knots in the thread ends, weave in, and cut (figure 14).

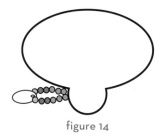

figure 14

66 Repeat steps 62 through 65 for the other side in mirror image.

67 Take the two remaining aqua terra sections. Use the one with the Herringbone Loop on the right. Repeat step 53, except count down nine beads in a counterclockwise direction and loop through the previously attached section on the right. Use the remaining section and repeat step 53, except count down nine beads in a clockwise direction and loop through the previously attached section on the left.

68 Cut 2½ yards (2.3 m) of thread and put a needle on. Move the needle to the center to work double thread.

69 Repeat step 65, except start just under the Herringbone Loop toward the necklace center and end at the loop on the other side.

70 Take the two tiger jasper sections. Use the one with the loop on the right. Repeat step 53, except count down seven beads in a counterclockwise direction and loop through the previously attached section on the right. Use the remaining section and repeat step 53, except count down seven beads in a clockwise direction and loop through the previously attached section on the left.

71 Cut 2 yards (1.8 m) of thread and put a needle on. Move the needle to the center to work double thread.

72 Repeat step 65, except use two tan beads in the loop instead of three, and start just under the Herringbone Loop toward the necklace center, and end at the loop on the other side.

73 Use the jump rings to attach the hook to one end loop and the eye to the other.

Sandy Spivey

Treasures of the Mermaid, 2010

Pendant, 17.5 cm long

Seed beads, shells, copper findings, chain,
Czech daggers, crystals, hex beads

Lee Wilkins

Untitled, 2010

11.4 x 6.4 x 1.3 cm

Seed beads, aventurine, carnelian
agate, oolitic jasper, black onyx

Arline Lewis

Beach, 2010

3.5 x 22 cm

Shell, seed beads, bugle beads

Judy Knight

Untitled, 2010

12.7 x 15.2 cm

Seed beads, bugle beads, pinch beads, crystals, goldstone, dichroic beads by Paula Radke, beaded beads by Leslie Froger

Sandra Kano

The "S", 2010

7.6 x 10.2 cm

Seed beads, pearls, crystals, drops, blister pearls,
flower crystals, mother-of-pearl beads

Sandy Wetzstein

Captured Copper, 2010

8.9 x 5.1 x 0.6 cm

Seed beads, copper wire

Arline Lewis

Ocean Currents Necklace, 2010

10 x 21 cm

Ocean jasper, pearls,
seed beads, chain

LEFT
Kandra Norsigian
Three Fish and More, 2010
16.5 x 11.4 x 1.3 cm
Seed beads, jade fish,
ceramic tile, drops

BELOW
Karin L. Salomon
Desert and Sea, 2010
17.8 x 7.6 cm
Turquoise cabochons,
seed beads, bugle beads

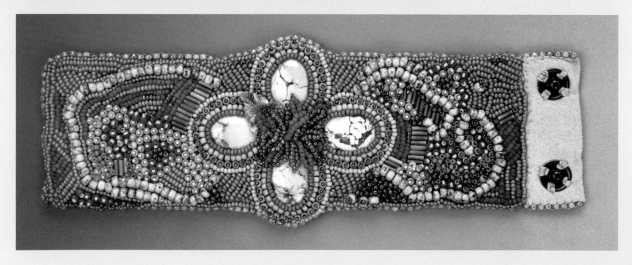

ABOVE
Yvonne Cabalona
Mom, 2010
7.6 x 10.8 cm

Freshwater pearls, peridot drop
bead, Czech glass, seed beads

RIGHT
Yvonne Cabalona
Lady in Red, 2010
11.5 x 10.2 cm

Mother-of-pearl, Czech glass,
black onyx, seed beads

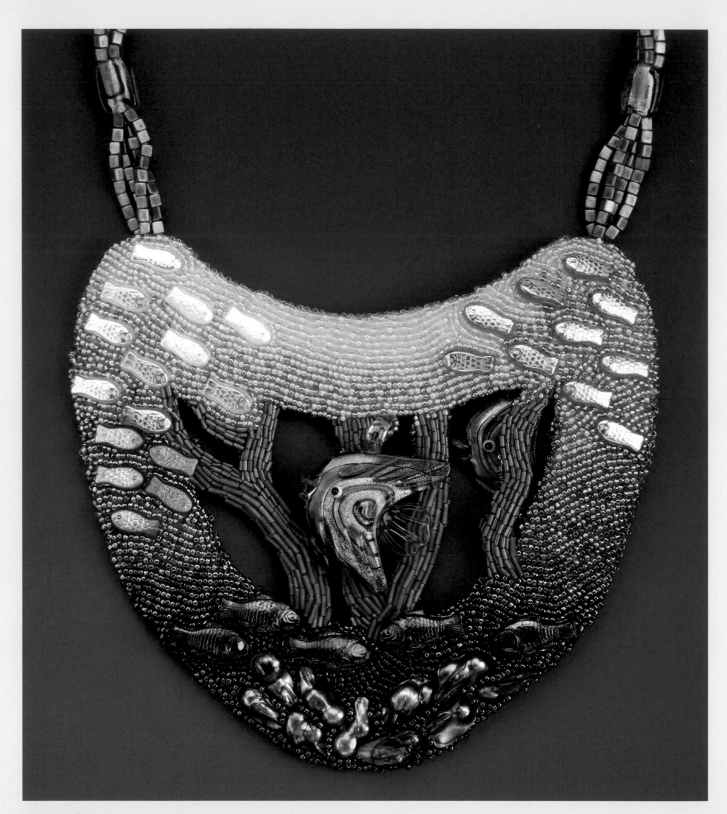

Diane Mahan

Under the Sea, 2010
12.7 x 17.8 x 1.3 cm

Seed beads, pearls, glass pendants, cubes, and other glass beads

Lee Wilkins

Summer Daze, 2010
6.6 x 6.6 x 1 cm

Seed beads, mother-of-pearl,
pressed glass, opalite

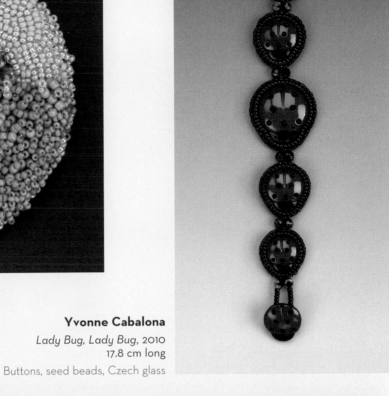

Yvonne Cabalona

Lady Bug, Lady Bug, 2010
17.8 cm long

Buttons, seed beads, Czech glass

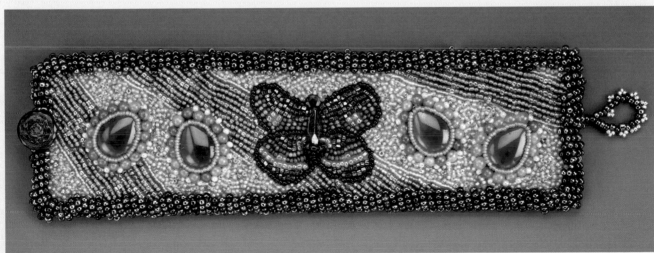

Juanita Dodd Robinson

Rain Forest, 2010
5 x 21 cm

Seed beads, aventurine, antique teardrops,
seed pearls, black crystal

Arline Lewis

Forest Deep, 2010
3.5 x 22 cm

Turquoise cabochons, seed beads, pearls

Cathie Schultze

Serenity, 2010
16 x 14 cm

Turquoise cabochon, turquoise donut, onyx rounds,
garnet rondelles, garnet beads, smoky quartz,
turquoise beads, dark green druk beads, black stone,
turquoise, black crystals, seed beads

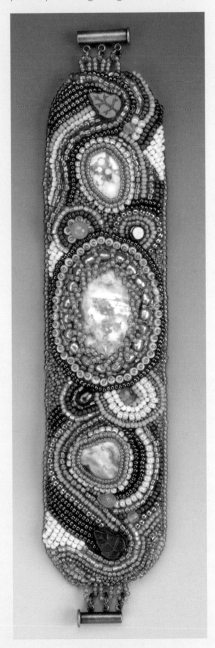

Arline Lewis

Ocean Currents Cuff, 2010

3.5 x 22 cm

Ocean jasper cabochons, seed beads, pearls, pressed glass, gemstone chips

Susan Stewart

Untitled, 2010

22 x 12 cm

Seed beads, Czech glass, bone and stone fetishes, polymer clay face, vintage glass tulip beads

Pam Killingsworth

The Rivers Edge, 2010
10 x 16 x 0.5 cm
Lampwork glass cabochon by Pam Killingsworth, Brazilian agate, seed beads, stone chips

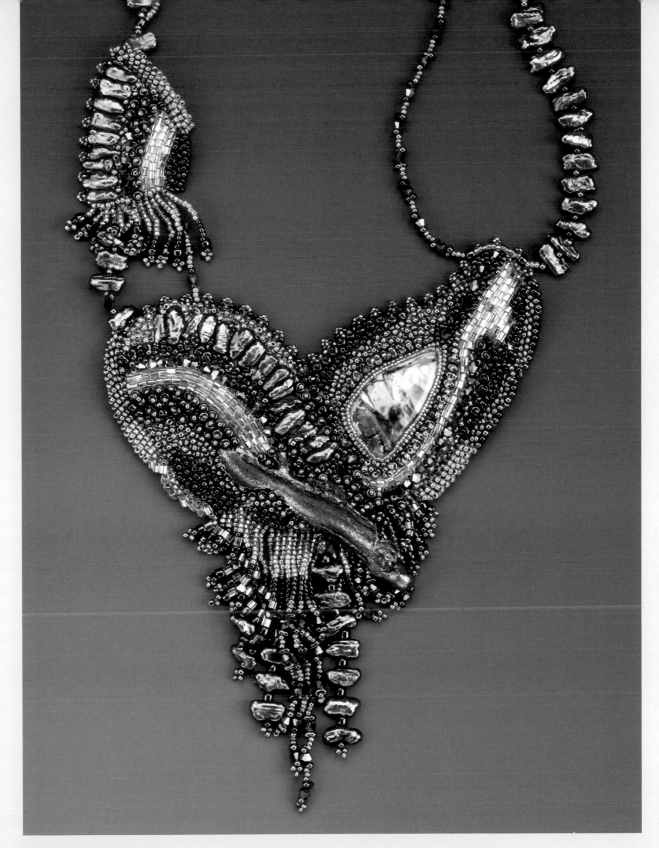

Susan Terese McKechnie

Tiffany and Titanium, 2010

Pendant, 23 x 18 cm

Bertrandite cabochon, titanium crystal, seed beads, freshwater pearls, crystals

Photo Descriptions

* indicates a technique from *Beading with Cabochons* by Jamie Cloud Eakin.

** indicates a technique from *Beading with Cabochons* by Jamie Cloud Eakin that is also illustrated in this book as part of the free-form edge, figure 31 on page 75.

Page 2 (also see page 32, center): Turquoise (40-mm and 50-mm donuts), tiger-eye (8-mm round cabochons), turquoise beads, tiger-eye beads. Standard bezel, backstitch, couch stitch, one-bead stitch, stacks stitch, fringe, sunshine edge, sunshine edge (picot variation).

Page 3, see project on page 90.

Page 5, top: See page 64, right.

Page 5, center (also see page 66, right): Muscovite (25 x 40-mm bead and carved leaf drop bead), oolitic jasper (16 x 40-mm bead). Standard bezel, backstitch, fringe drop, crown points edge, herringbone loop bail attachment.

Page 5, bottom: See page 34, top left.

Page 14, left (also see page 38, center): Glass beads. Standard bezel, backstitch, lazy stitch, stacks stitch, one-bead stitch, side petal edge, fringe, herringbone loop bail attachment.

Page 14, center (also see page 39): Lampwork glass cabochon (30 x 42 mm) by Pam Killingsworth. Standard bezel, backstitch, stacks stitch, backstitch layer, side petal edge, direct attachment*.

Page 14, right (also see page 59, right; page 82, top left): Amazonite (25 x 38-mm bead), serpentine carved rose (25-mm bead). Bugle row and outside window bezel combination, standard bezel, couch stitch, backstitch, combining, fringe, sunshine edge, square stitch bail attachment.

Page 16, left (also see page 33, top second from left): Crazy lace agate (32 x 40-mm oval donut), picture jasper (18 x 12-mm and 8-mm beads). Standard bezel, backstitch, stacks stitch, loop stitch, fringe, sunshine edge, herringbone loop bail attachment.

Page 16, right (also see page 44, right): Faceted pointed-back crystal pendant (26 x 46-mm marquis). Outside window bezel, stacks stitch, picot stitch, backstitch, chain-o-beads stitch, fringe, sunshine edge, direct attachment*.

Page 17, right column, left: Porcelain cabochon center. Standard bezel, backstitch, stacks stitch, picot stitch, clover stitch, wave edge.

Page 17, right column, right (also see page 46, left): Metal finding center. Backstitch, braid stitch, clean edge.

Page 20, left: Botswana agate beads (25 x 30-mm rectangle and 24 x 18-mm oval). One-bead stitch, backstitch, circles edge, herringbone loop bail attachment.

Page 20, second from left: Botswana agate beads (25 x 30-mm rectangle and 24 x 18-mm oval). One-bead stitch, backstitch, combining, points edge**, side bead attachment.

Page 20, third from left: Dichroic glass cabochons. Standard bezel, backstitch, stacks stitch, side petal edge, fringe, square stitch bail attachment.

Page 20, right: Dichroic glass cabochons. Standard bezel, backstitch, combining, fringe, sunshine edge, square stitch bail attachment.

Page 21, top left: Carnelian agate flower bead (45 mm), unakite cabochons (8-mm round) and leaf beads (12 x 17-mm), red agate cabochons. One-bead stitch, backstitch, fringe, wave edge, sunshine edge, combining, layering.

Page 21, top center: Ocean jasper, moukaite, rhyolite, and rhodonite beads. One-bead stitch, standard bezel, backstitch, picot stitch, branch fringe, combining, sunshine edge, points edge**, direct attachment*.

Page 21, top right: Malachite cabochons, beads, uncut mineral, brass statuette. Standard bezel, one-bead stitch, backstitch, points edge**, sunshine edge, fringe, added bead attachment.

Page 21, bottom left (also see page 70, second from left): Calcite, moukaite, and cream quartz beads/cabochons. Carved bone bead drop. Window bezel*, standard bezel, backstitch, couch stitch, fringe, circles edge, points edge**, combining, direct attachment*.

Page 21, bottom center: Kyanite beads (62 x 10-mm oval, 45 x 10-mm oval, and 16 x 42-mm teardrop). Standard (bead-raised) bezel, backstitch, couch stitch, combining, sunshine edge, square stitch bail attachment.

Page 21, bottom right (also see page 49, left): Fancy jasper (8-mm to 20 x 30-mm round cabochons). Standard bezel, combining, branch fringe, points edge**, direct attachment.*

Page 26, left: Leopardskin jasper (21 x 45-mm teardrop pendant and 15 x 20-mm rectangle bead). Twisted bezel, one-bead stitch, backstitch, couch stitch, stacks stitch, sunshine edge, square stitch bail attachment.

Page 26, right: See page 56, center.

Page 27, top left: Agate slice pendant, mahogany obsidian bead, metal statuette. Standard bezel, backstitch, layering, points edge**, added bead attachment.

Page 27, top center: Kyanite pendant. Standard bezel, backstitch, points edge**, ladder stitch bail attachment*.

Page 27, top right: Horn top-drilled beads, black onyx cabochons, Dalmatian jasper cabochons, bone and wood beads. Standard bezel, one-bead stitch, backstitch, picot stitch, stacks stitch, loop fringe, sunshine edge, combining.

Page 27, bottom left: Artist paintbrush jasper (32 x 65-mm pendant). Standard bezel, backstitch, clean edge, square stitch bail attachment.

Page 27, bottom right: Bone (45 x 60-mm paisley/teardrop pendant), black onyx (8 x 12-mm cabochon). Standard bezel, backstitch, crown points edge, herringbone loop bail attachment.

Page 28, top left: Agate slice (60 x 40-mm pendant). Standard bezel, backstitch, twisted edge*.

Page 28, top second from left: Agate slice (45 x 60-mm pendant). Standard bezel, backstitch, sunshine edge, ladder stitch bail attachment*, drop with crystal and peyote stitch.

Page 28, top third from left: Artist paintbrush jasper (35 x 65-mm pendant). Window bezel*, backstitch, sunshine edge, added bead attachment.

Page 28, top right: Turquoise (30-mm round pendant). Standard (bead-raised) bezel, couch stitch, backstitch, points edge**.

Page 28, bottom (also see page 62 and page 70, right): Turquoise oval cabochon, magnesite cabochons, turquoise teardrop pendants. Standard bezel, backstitch, combining, circles edge.

Page 29, left: Rivolis (27-mm triangle, 15 x 20-mm oval, 12-mm round, and 20-mm round). Standard (bead-raised) bezel, couch stitch, backstitch, side petal edge, square stitch bail attachment.

Page 29, center: Rivoli (12-mm round). Standard (bead-raised) bezel, backstitch, backstitch layers, fringe, sunshine edge, direct attachment*.

Page 29, right: Rivolis (12-mm and 16-mm rounds). Standard (bead-raised) bezel, couch stitch, backstitch, side petal edge.

Page 30, left: Various beads and buttons. One-bead stitch, backstitch, picot stitch, lazy stitch, loop stitch, rope edge. Sewn onto a purse made from the bottom of the leg of an old pair of jeans, using the belt loops for the loops on the purse and the inseam for the purse strap.

Page 30, second from left: Vintage buttons (42-mm, 32-mm, and 18-mm rounds). Standard (bead-raised) bezel, couch stitch, backstitch, one-bead stitch, sunshine edge, fringe, points edge**, direct attachment*.

Page 30, third from left: Button (18-mm round shank type), rivolis (12 mm). Standard (bead-raised) bezel, stacks stitch, backstitch, side petal edge, combining.

Page 30, right: Button (23-mm regular style). One-bead stitch, backstitch, sunshine edge, direct attachment*.

Page 32, left: Fossil (45-mm donut), hematite (10-mm round cabochon). Window bezel*, couch stitch, backstitch, points edge**, sunshine edge (picot variation), added bead attachment.

Page 32, center: See page 2.

Page 32, right: Red aventurine (40-mm donut), mahogany obsidian (10-mm round cabochon). Standard (bead-raised) bezel, couch stitch, backstitch, fringe, points edge**, sunshine edge (picot variation), added bead attachment.

Page 33, top left: Aventurine donuts (25 mm and 15 mm). Standard bezel, backstitch, stacks stitch, fringe, sunshine edge, direct attachment*.

Page 33, top second from left: See page 16, left.

Page 33, top third from left: Aventurine (15-mm donuts). Standard bezel, one-bead stitch, couch stitch, backstitch, picot stitch, stacks stitch, lazy stitch, clean edge.

Page 33, top right: Glass donut (50 mm), goldstone (13 x 18-mm, 15 x 30-mm, and 10-mm cabochons). Standard bezel, couch stitch, backstitch, stacks stitch with branch fringe, lazy edge.

Page 33, bottom left: Foil glass (38-mm donut), lampwork cabochon (30 mm), vintage button (16-mm shank style). Bead-across bezel with a flower stitch in the middle, standard bezel, backstitch, side petal edge, points edge**, fringe, added bead attachment.

Page 33, bottom center: Sodalite (35 x 52-mm rectangle donut), lapis bead. Bead-cross and standard bezel combination, backstitch, one-bead stitch, stacks stitch, fringe, sunshine edge, added bead attachment.

Page 33, bottom right: Dichroic glass (42-mm donut), goldstone cabochon. Standard (bead-raised) bezel, backstitch, couch stitch, picot stitch, fringe, side petal edge, sunshine edge, direct attachment*.

Page 34, top left (also see page 5, bottom): Ammonite half (42 x 55 mm). Standard (bead-raised) bezel, beads of varying size around the ammonite, backstitch, branch fringe, points edge**, added bead attachment.

Page 34, top second from left: Prenite and copper mineral, aventurine cabochon. One-bead stitch, couch stitch, standard bezel, fringe, points edge**, added bead attachment.

Page 34, top third from left: Vanadinite mineral (35 x 30 mm), jade (42 x 15-mm oval cabochon). Standard bezel, backstitch, combining, sunshine edge, added bead attachment.

Page 34, top right: Unpolished pyrite, hematite cabochons. Standard bezel, couch stitch, backstitch, combining, fringe, points edge**, added bead attachment.

Page 34, bottom left: Red agate pendant of Quan Yin, striped agate bead, carnelian cabochon, carnelian leaf beads. Standard bezel, backstitch, one-bead stitch, couch stitch, points edge**, added bead attachment.

Page 34, bottom second from left: Cat's-eye (8-mm, 12-mm, and 14-mm round cabochons). Standard bezel, layering, fringe, combining, sunshine edge (picot variation).

Page 34, bottom third from left: Serpentine cabochons. Standard bezel, backstitch, layering, combining, fringe, points edge**, direct attachment*.

Page 34, bottom right: Glass cabochon with backing image of a cat. Standard bezel, backstitch, fringe, points edge**, ladder stitch bail attachment*.

Page 35, see page 36, center.

Page 36, left: Cloisonné beads (30 x 40 mm). One-bead stitch, backstitch, fringe, sunshine edge, direct attachment*.

Page 36, center (also see page 35): Bone, horn, mother-of-pearl beads. One-bead stitch, backstitch, couch stitch, stacks stitch, fringe, sunshine edge, direct attachment*.

Page 36, right: Stick pearl beads and freshwater pearl beads. One bead stitch, backstitch, fringe, sunshine edge, direct attachment*.

Page 37, left top: Clay face cabochon. Standard bezel, backstitch, stacks stitch, side petal edge.

Page 37, left bottom: Mother-of-pearl beads. One-bead stitch, backstitch, stacks stitch, picot stitch, lazy stitch, clean edge.

Page 37, right: Ocean jasper slices. Bead-across bezel, backstitch, stacks stitch, loop fringe, sunshine edge, direct attachment*.

Page 38, left: Glass bead. Stacks stitch, backstitch, fringe, sunshine edge, added bead attachment.

Page 38, center: See page 14, left.

Page 38, right: Fancy jasper cabochons. Standard bezel, couch stitch, backstitch, one-bead stitch, points edge**, fringe, added bead attachment.

Page 39, see page 14, center.

Page 40, left: Crystal bicones (4 mm). Couch stitch, backstitch, sunshine edge, combining, fringe, direct attachment*.

Page 40, center: Glass foil beads. Standard (bead-raised) bezel, couch stitch, backstitch, combining, fringe, points edge**, direct attachment*.

Page 40, right: Dichroic glass (15 x 22-mm cabochons). Standard (bead-raised) bezel, couch stitch, backstitch, combining, side petal edge, sunshine edge, direct attachment*.

Page 41, left: Cameo (25 x 34-mm cabochon), goldstone (15 x 28-mm and 8-mm cabochons), aragonite crystal cluster. Standard bezel, backstitch, backstitch layer, picot stitch, stacks stitch, fringe, sunshine edge, direct attachment*.

Page 41, center: Green opal beads 32-mm triangle, 20 x 40-mm oval, 13 x 18-mm oval. Standard bezel (bead-raised), backstitch, couch stitch, picot stitch, combining, fringe, sunshine edge, direct attachment*.

Page 41, right: Dichroic glass (12 x 15-mm cabochon). Standard (bead-raised) bezel, couch stitch, backstitch, picot stitch, sunshine edge, top loop attachment*.

Page 42, left: Crystal points cluster. Loop stitch, picot stitch, one-bead stitch, backstitch, fringe, side petal edge, square stitch bail attachment.

Page 42, right top: Ultrasuede pouch, glass beads. Loop stitch, stacks stitch, one-bead stitch.

Page 42, right bottom: Seed beads. Picot stitch, loop stitch, backstitch.

Page 43, left: See page 78, left.

Page 43, center: See page 58, center.

Page 43, right: Seed beads. Lazy stitch, free-form edge.

Page 44, left: Hat band made of ribbon, attached with a hematite cabochon pin. Chain-o-beads stitch, sunshine edge with 4-mm bead variation.

Page 44, center: Fire-polished beads (4 mm), seed beads. Chain-o-beads stitch, backstitch, sunshine edge.

Page 44, right: See page 16, right.

Page 45, left: Ocean jasper (20 x 40-mm marquis bead), fossilized coral (18 x 25-mm bead). Standard (bead-raised) bezel, couch stitch, backstitch, clover stitch, stacks stitch, fringe, side petal edge, direct attachment*.

Page 45, center: Black onyx (8 x 22-mm cabochon). Standard bezel, backstitch, clover stitch, sunshine edge, direct attachment*.

Page 45, right: Glass beads. Clover stitch, backstitch, lazy stitch, picot stitch, stacks stitch, sunshine edge.

Page 46, left: See page 17 right column, right.

Page 46, center: Turquoise (52-mm donut), tiger-eye (8-mm round cabochon), serpentine (20 x 25-mm cabochon). Standard bezel, bead-across bezel, layering, backstitch, braid stitch, lazy stitch, sunshine edge, direct attachment*.

Page 46, right: Glass beads. One-bead stitch, backstitch, braid stitch, wave edge.

Page 48, See page 58, right.

Page 49, left: See page 21, bottom right.

Page 49, right: Porcelain (42 x 75-mm teardrop cabochon). Standard bezel, backstitch, loop fringe, points edge**, added bead attachment.

Page 50, left top: Jasper (35 x 45-mm cabochon). Outside window bezel, couch stitch, backstitch, crown points edge, herringbone loop bail attachment.

Page 50, left bottom, and center: Dichroic glass (22 x 25-mm cabochon). Outside window bezel, couch stitch, backstitch, fringe, side petal edge, square stitch bail attachment.

Page 50, right: Foil glass (16 x 24 mm), vintage glass (14 x 18-mm cabochon). Outside window bezel, standard bezel, couch stitch, backstitch, fringe, side petal edge, herringbone loop bail attachment.

Page 52, left: White aventurine (32 x 40-mm cabochon). Twisted bezel, backstitch, points edge**, added bead attachment.

Page 52, center: Turquoise (36 x 45-mm teardrop bead). Outside window twisted bezel, backstitch, couch stitch, points edge**, square stitch bail attachment.

Page 52, right: Fossil stone (30 x 40-mm cabochon). Twisted bezel, backstitch, loop fringe, side petal edge, added bead attachment.

Page 54, left: Montana agate (28 x 38 mm), amethyst sage agate (40 x 50 mm), black obsidian (14 mm). Stacks bezel, bead-across bezel, backstitch, picot stitch, sunshine edge, added bead attachment.

Page 54, center: Rivolis (16 mm, 18 mm, and 27 mm). Stacks bezel, stacks stitch, backstitch, fringe, sunshine edge, side petal edge, direct attachment*.

Page 54, right (also see page 55): Rivolis (12 mm, 16 mm, and 18 mm). Stacks bezel, picot stitch, combining, sunshine edge, direct attachment*.

Page 55, see page 54, right.

Page 56, left: White plume agate (35 x 48 mm). Bugle row bezel, backstitch, fringe, sunshine edge, herringbone loop bail attachment.

Page 56, center (also see page 26, right): Abalone pendant. Bugle row bezel, backstitch, sunshine edge, square stitch bail attachment.

Page 56, right: Montana agate (20 x 23 mm). Bugle row bezel, couch stitch, picot stitch, sunshine edge, side petal edge, direct attachment*.

Page 58, left (also see page 65): Owyhee jasper (35 x 55 mm), red creek jasper (18 x 25 mm). Bead-across bezel, backstitch, one-bead stitch, stacks stitch, picot stitch, sunshine edge, sunshine edge with 4-mm variation, square stitch bail attachment.

Page 58, center (also see page 43, center): Dichroic glass (25 x 37-mm pendant), mountain jade (8-mm round cabochon). Bead-across bezel, standard bezel, backstitch, lazy stitch, sunshine edge, sunshine edge (picot variation), square stitch bail attachment.

Page 58, right (see also page 48): Malachite and copper (30 x 60-mm slice), green quartz (30 x 18-mm Quan Yin pendant). Bead-across bezel, standard bezel, backstitch, lazy stitch, picot stitch, loop fringe, sunshine edge, combining.

Page 59, left: Ammonite half (32 x 40 mm). Standard and outside window bezel combination, couch stitch, backstitch, points edge**, added bead attachment.

Page 59, center: See page 73, left.

Page 59, right: See page 14, right.

Page 60, left: Plume agate (36 x 50-mm cabochon). Flower and standard bezel combination, couch stitch, clean edge, herringbone loop bail attachment.

Page 60, center: White aventurine (32 x 45-mm cabochon). Flower bezel, backstitch, fringe, side petal edge, herringbone loop bail attachment.

Page 60, right: Mother-of-pearl (15 x 20-mm flat oval bead). Bead-across and flower bezel combination, backstitch, fringe, points edge**.

Page 62, see page 28, bottom.

Page 63, left: Graphic feldspar (51 x 68-mm cabochon). Standard bezel, backstitch, clean edge, herringbone loop bail attachment.

Page 63, second from left: Crazy lace agate (50-mm bead). Standard bezel, backstitch, clean edge, herringbone loop bail attachment.

Page 63, third from left: Baroque pearls. One-bead stitch, backstitch, stacks stitch, lazy stitch, picot stitch, clean edge.

Page 63, right: Ammonite half (22 x 30 mm). Standard (bead-raised) bezel, backstitch, clean edge, direct attachment*.

Page 64, left: Mustard aventurine Zuni bear pendant. Bead-across bezel, standard bezel, backstitch, sunshine edge, ladder stitch bail attachment*.

Page 64, center: Serpentine (30 x 40-mm marquis beads). Standard bezel, backstitch, fringe, combining, sunshine edge, direct attachment*.

Page 64, right (see also page 5, top). Kyanite (15 x 20-mm bead), pewter butterfly pendant. Standard (bead-raised) bezel, couch stitch, backstitch, one-bead stitch, sunshine edge, direct attachment*.

Page 65, see page 58, left.

Page 66, left: Hemimorphite (30 x 40-mm bead), painted wood leaf bead. Standard bezel, backstitch, crown points edge, fringe drop, top loop bail attachment*.

Page 66, center: Zebra jasper (26 x 30-mm bead). Standard bezel, backstitch, crown points edge, square stitch bail attachment.

Page 66, right: See page 5, center.

Page 67, left: Amazonite (20 x 30-mm bead). Standard bezel, couch stitch, backstitch, side petal edge, fringed turn attachment.

Page 67, center: Agate (75 x 42-mm slice). Standard bezel, backstitch, side petal edge, square stitch bail attachment, herringbone loop bail attachment.

Page 67, right: Sodalite (20 x 30-mm cabochon). Standard bezel, backstitch, side petal edge, fringe, added bead attachment.

Page 68, left: Dyed quartz, (32-mm bead). Standard bezel, backstitch, rope edge with drop, square stitch bail attachment.

Page 68, center: Petrified wood (55 x 70-mm slice). Bead-across bezel, backstitch, sunshine edge, rope edge and side petal edge combination, direct attachment*.

Page 68, right: Dichroic glass (12 x 15-mm cabochon). Standard bezel, rope edge with middle bead variation, back side bead attachment*.

Page 70, left: Chinese flower jade (26 x 36-mm bead). Standard and window bezel* combination, backstitch, circles edge, ladder stitch bail attachment*.

Page 70, second from left: See page 21, bottom left.

Page 70, third from left: Bamboo agate (26 x 35-mm bead). Standard bezel, backstitch, circles edge, added bead attachment.

Page 70, right: See page 28, bottom.

Page 71, left: Aquamarine (18 x 22-mm nugget bead). Standard (bead-raised) bezel, couch stitch, backstitch, lace ruffle edge, ladder stitch bail attachment*.

Page 71, center: Coin pearl (10-mm bead). Standard bezel, couch stitch, backstitch, lace ruffle edge, added bead attachment.

Page 71, right top: Glass (35 x 40-mm cabochon) with cat image behind it. Standard bezel, backstitch, lace ruffle edge.

Page 71, right bottom: Rivoli (12 mm). Standard bezel, backstitch, lace ruffle edge.

Page 73, left (also see page 59, center): Rutilated quartz (20 x 25 mm, 10 x 15 mm, and 7 x 10 mm). Standard and outside window bezel combination, standard bezel, one-bead stitch, picot stitch, backstitch, wave edge, herringbone loop bail attachment.

Page 73, center: Montana agate (28 x 38-mm cabochon), black onyx (14-mm and 8-mm cabochons). Standard bezel, backstitch, wave edge.

Page 73, right: Ocean jasper (30-mm round and 24 x 28-mm rectangle beads). Outside window bezel, couch stitch, backstitch, combining, wave edge, ladder stitch bail attachment*.

Page 75, left: Orange calcite (22 x 42-mm) bead. Standard bezel, couch stitch, backstitch, free-form edge, fringed turn attachment.

Page 75, center: Mountain jade (10-mm cabochons) over mother-of-pearl (14-mm beads). Standard bezel, one-bead stitch, backstitch, layering, sunshine edge (picot variation), free-form edge.

Page 75, right: Rose quartz (25-mm cabochon). Standard bezel, couch stitch, backstitch, free-form edge, added bead attachment.

Page 77, left: Crazy lace agate (30-mm bead). Standard bezel, couch stitch, backstitch, one-bead stitch, picot stitch, lazy stitch, fringe, sunshine edge, direct attachment*.

Page 77, center: Ocean jasper (25 x 36-mm bead). Standard bezel, backstitch, loop fringe, points edge**, added bead attachment.

Page 77, right: Black onyx (20 x 28-mm, 18-mm, and 8-mm cabochons). Standard bezel, backstitch, combining, fringe.

Page 78, left (also see page 43, left): Scarab beads, turquoise chips. Standard (bead-raised) bezel, couch stitch, backstitch, stacks stitch, lazy stitch, lazy edge.

Page 78, center: Striped agate (23 x 48-mm bead). Loop stitch, picot stitch, lazy edge, back side bead attachment*.

Page 78, right: Serpentine (10-mm butterflies), coral (6-mm round beads). One-bead stitch, lazy stitch, clover stitch, lazy edge.

Page 79, see page 82, bottom left.

Page 80, left: Sodalite (24 x 28-mm bead). Standard bezel, backstitch, crown points edge, herringbone loop bail attachment.

Page 80, second from left: Turquoise (15 x 42-mm marquis cabochon). Standard bezel, backstitch, sunshine edge, herringbone loop bail attachment.

Page 80, third from left: Cloisonné (32 x 56-mm bead). Standard (bead-raised) bezel, couch stitch, backstitch, sunshine edge, herringbone loop bail attachment.

Page 80, right: Chinese flower jade (26 x 38-mm bead). Standard bezel, backstitch, loop fringe, points edge**, herringbone loop bail attachment.

Page 82, top left: See page 14, right.

Page 82, top second from left: Agate (32 x 42-mm cabochon). Standard bezel, backstitch, points edge**, square stitch bail attachment.

Page 82, top third from left: Dichroic glass (28 x 34-mm cabochon). Outside window bezel, couch stitch, backstitch, sunshine edge, square stitch bail attachment.

Page 82, top right: Goldstone (50-mm carved rose pendant). Standard bezel, backstitch, clean edge, square stitch bail attachment.

Page 82, bottom left (also see page 79): Lime chalk turquoise (32 x 50-mm cabochon). Standard bezel, backstitch, fringe, sunshine edge, square stitch bail attachment.

Page 82, bottom center: Ocean jasper (25 x 30-mm bead), serpentine (15-mm square cabochon). Standard bezel, backstitch, couch stitch, combining, fringe, points edge**, square stitch bail attachment.

Page 82, bottom right: Lime chalk turquoise (22 x 52-mm cabochon). Standard bezel, backstitch, sunshine edge, fringe, square stitch bail attachment.

Page 85, left: Plume agate (20 x 26-mm cabochon). Standard bezel, backstitch, turn bead edge* with drop, added bead attachment.

Page 85, second from left: Serpentine (24 x 32-mm bead). Twisted bezel, backstitch, fringe, points edge**, added bead attachment.

Page 85, third from left: Botswana agate (32 x 42-mm bead). Standard bezel, backstitch, fringe drop, points edge**, added bead attachment.

Page 85, right: Picasso jasper (30 x 40-mm bead). Standard bezel, backstitch, fringe drop, sunshine edge, added bead attachment on the sides with drops.

Page 86, Ocean jasper (25 x 28-mm bead). Standard (bead-raised) bezel, couch stitch, backstitch, rope edge, added bead attachment.

Page 87, left: Pink lepidolite (30-mm bead). Standard bezel, backstitch, turn bead edge* with drop, fringed turn attachment.

Page 87, second from left: Assembled black obsidian and mother-of-pearl (30 x 38-mm bead). Standard bezel, backstitch, lace ruffle edge, fringed turn attachment.

Page 87, third from left: Striped agate (20 x 26-mm bead). Standard bezel, backstitch, turn bead edge* with drop, fringed turn attachment.

Page 87, right: Ocean jasper (22 x 28-mm bead). Standard (bead-raised) bezel, couch stitch, backstitch, side petal edge, fringed turn attachment.

Acknowledgments

I want to acknowledge and thank bead groups everywhere. From small two-person groups to large organized groups, and even large unorganized groups of beaders—also known as customers at a bead show!—you inspire me and enrich my life. We may all be different, with a variety of points of view, incomes, family situations, etc., but we put it all aside and unite in our passion for beads and beadwork. It seems that beading brings out the best in all of us.

I also want to thank a special beader, Candace Cloud McLean, for sharing my obsession and giving me support. And, without a doubt, thank you to my husband, Stephen, who encourages me to be all I can be and doesn't mind that I often interpret that as *bead all I can bead.*

About the Author

Jamie Cloud Eakin has been a professional bead artist for almost two decades, and she teaches and sells her work in galleries across North America. She's the author of *Beading with Cabochons* and *Bugle Bead Bonanza.* Jamie lives in Modesto, California. Her website is www.StudioJamie.com.

PHOTO BY McLEAN DESIGN

Index